SOLAR SYSTEM REFERENCE FOR TEENS

SOLAR SYSTEM SYSTEM REFERENCE FOR TEENS

A FASCINATING GUIDE TO OUR
PLANETS, MOONS, SPACE PROGRAMS,
AND MORE

BRUCE BETTS, PhD

ROCKRIDGE
PRESS

First Rockridge Press trade paperback edition 2022

Rockridge Press and the Rockridge Press logo are trademarks or registered trademarks of Callisto Media Inc. and/or its affiliates in the United States and other countries and may not be used without written permission.

For general information on our other products and services, please contact our Customer Care Department within the United States at (866) 744-2665, or outside the United States at (510) 253-0500.

Paperback ISBN: 978-1-63878-738-9
eBook ISBN: 978-1-63878-945-1

Manufactured in the United States of America

Interior and Cover Designer: Tricia Jang
Art Producer: Sara Feinstein
Editor: Julie Haverkate
Production Editor: Ruth Sakata Corley
Production Manager: Lanore Coloprisco

Photograpy © Detlev van Ravenswaay/Science Source, p. ii; Shutterstock, cover, pps. v-ix, 19, 23-25, 74-75, 168; NASA/JPL, pps. x-1, 59, 66, 68, 79, 85, 89, 101, 104-105, 107-108, 110-111, 147; NASA, pps. x-1, 3, 6-7, 12, 14-15, 20, 31, 34, 41, 43, 45, 47, 51-52, 74-75, 96, 129, 140, 142, 146, 153, 162, 172; Mark Garlick/Science Source, p. 2; NASA/Lunar and Planetary Institute, p. 9; Alamy, p. 10, 16, 22, 32, 37, 46, 53, 64, 73, 113, 118-119, 123-124, 126, 141, 145, 167; NASA Imagine the Universe, p. 11; NASA/SDO, p. 13, 19; ESA/Hubble & NASA, J. Kalirai, p. 17; NASA/GSFC/SDO, p. 17; NASA/SDO/GSFC, p. 19; Bruce Betts, p. 22; NASA/JHUAPL, p. 24; NASA/JPL-Caltech, p. 24, 33, 58, 60, 97; NASA/Apollo 17 crew, p. 24; ESA/MPS/UPD/LAM/IAA/RSSD/INTA/UPM/DASP/IDA, pps. 24-25; NASA / JHUAPL / CIW, p. 26, 28, 31; NASA/Johns Hopkins University Applied Physics Laboratory/Carnegie Institution of Washington, p. 27; NASA's Goddard Space Flight Center, p. 30; ESA/MPS/DLR/IDA, p. 34; Russian Space Agency, p. 36; NASA/JPL, p. 36, 38, 39; NASA EPIC, p. 42; NASA/NOAA, p. 42; USGS, p. 44; NASA/JPL/USGS, p. 49, 54, 106, 115; NASA/Eugene Cernan, p. 50; Philip James/Steven Lee/NASA, p. 55; NASA/JPL-Caltech/ASU, p. 56; NASA/JPL/JHUAPL/MSSS/Brown U., p. 57; NASA/JPL-Caltech/MSSS, p. 58; NASA/JPL-Caltech/U. of Arizona, p. 62-63, 76, 83; NASA/JPL-Caltech/UCLA/MPS/DLR/IDA, p. 65; ESA/Hubble, M. Kornmesser, p. 65; NASA / Goddard / University of Arizona, p. 68; NASA/JPL-Caltech/UCLA/MPS/DLR/IDA, p. 70, 72; NASA/JPL-Caltech/SwRI/MSSS/Kevin M. Gill, p. 77; NASA/JPL-Caltech/SwRI/MSSS/Betsy Asher Hall/Gervasio Robles, p. 78; NASA/JPL/Cornell University, p. 80; JPL/NASA/STScI, p. 80; NASA/JPL/DLR, p. 82; NASA/JPL-Caltech/Michael Carroll, p. 84; NASA/JPL/SSI, p. 86, 89; NASA/JPL/Space Science Institute, pps. 87-88, 90, 92, 95; NASA/JPL/University of Arizona/University of Idaho, p. 93; ESA/NASA/JPL/University of Arizona, p. 93, 152; NASA/JPL/STScI, p. 98, 103; NASA/LPI, p. 100, 110; Hubble Space Telescope/Karen Meech, p. 117; NASA/JHUAPL/SwRI, p. 118, 120, 122; ESA/Rosetta/NAVCAM, p. 126; Caltech/R. Hurt (IPAC), p. 128; NASA, ESA, M. Robberto (Space Telescope Science Institute/ESA) and the Hubble Space Telescope Orion Treasury Project Team, pps. 130-131, 163; Johns Hopkins University Applied Physics Laboratory, pps. 130-131, 148; N.A.Sharp, NOAO/NSO/Kitt Peak FTS/AURA/NSF, p. 135; ESO/J. Rameau, p. 136; NASA/STS-82 Crew Member, p. 137; NASA GSFC/CIL/Adriana Manrique Gutierrez, p. 138; NASA/Ames/JPL-Caltech, p. 139; NASA/Joel Kowsky, p. 139; NASA/NSSDC/NASM, p. 144; NASA/JPL-Caltech/UMD, p. 151; NASA/JHUAPL/SwRI, p. 153; NPS/M.Quinn, p. 157; iStock, p. 159; NPS/M.Quinn, p. 160; NASA, ESA, AURA/Caltech, Palomar Observatory, p. 163; Torben Hansen, p. 164; NASA illustration by Robert Simmon, p. 164; CTIO/NOIRLab/NSF/AURA/J. Fuentes, p. 165.

10 9 8 7 6 5 4 3 2 1 0

FOR MY SONS,
KEVIN AND DANIEL

CONTENTS

INTRODUCTION

Welcome to the solar system! I will be your tour guide on an awesome adventure through space. Join me as we have fun exploring all the cool stuff in our solar system.

I've been fascinated by space ever since I was a child, when I used to look up at the night sky and wonder what was out there. As a teenager, I became even more fascinated with the pictures captured by spacecraft. These included our first views of the surface of Mars and erupting volcanoes on Jupiter's moon Io. When I saw these images of other worlds, I was hooked.

After high school, I completed college degrees in physics and math and a PhD in planetary science. My scientific research focused on the surface of Mars and the moons of Jupiter. I became more and more interested in sharing the excitement of space with others. Now, I'm chief scientist of the Planetary Society, the largest space interest group in the world. And I write books about space!

This book contains in-depth information about the solar system and space exploration. You'll meet key figures in history, learn about careers in astronomy, uncover some of the solar system's biggest mysteries, and more.

You can read this book from front to back or skip to the sections that interest you the most. In most of the chapters, we travel from one location to the next, moving outward through the solar system. The final chapter includes brief histories of spacecraft exploration and tips for conducting your own night-sky astronomy. Along the way, you'll find lots of gorgeous images and amazing diagrams that bring distant places to life.

I hope this book fills you with wonder and a desire to learn even more about the wild, weird worlds of our solar system.

—*Bruce Betts, PhD*

The solar system

THE SOLAR SYSTEM AT A GLANCE

Our solar system is made up of the Sun and everything that goes around it. The Sun has 99.8 percent of the material in the entire solar system, so you could think of the solar system as the Sun plus a bunch of other stuff. That includes billions of objects, like **planets**, **dwarf planets**, **asteroids**, **comets**, **moons**, and distant bodies called **trans-Neptunian objects**. All these things were left over from the formation of the Sun. We'll take a close look at all of them in this book.

This chapter covers the origins of the solar system, its structure, and how it fits into the **universe**. We will explore the basics of gravity and find out what makes a planet. Then we will focus on the big body at the heart of it all: the Sun.

Get ready to start an incredible journey through the system we call home, the system where we all live. That's right! It's time to venture out into the solar system.

THE MILKY WAY

The Milky Way

Our Sun is one star among hundreds of billions of stars in the Milky Way galaxy. If you're in a location with dark skies, look up and you'll see a milky band of subtle white light. The ancient Greeks and Romans referred to that as the Milky Way. Only in the past century have we really understood that this light comes from the collection of stars that make up our galaxy.

We live in a barred spiral galaxy. It is relatively flat with arms that spiral out. At the center is a bar-shaped concentration of stars. The Milky Way is about 100,000 **light-years** across. In other words, it takes light about 100,000 years to travel from one side of our galaxy to the other. And if that weren't mind-blowing enough, there are hundreds of billions of galaxies in our universe.

SOLAR SYSTEM ORIGINS

Gravity is the force that keeps your feet on the ground and causes a ball to drop when you throw it in the air. Anything that has mass also has gravity. Around 4.5 billion years ago, gas and dust were spread over a very large area of space. Gravity started pulling them closer. Slowly, all gas and dust in the area came together in a gravitational party. The center of this party eventually became the Sun, and the leftover materials became planets and other objects.

This theory of how the solar system formed is called the nebular hypothesis. It partly originated in the late 1700s and has evolved over the past few hundred years as people compared this theory to newer observations.

Everything in the solar system is rotating and revolving. To understand why, let's go back to the gas-and-dust party. As material started to pull inward, any small rotation in this giant cloud of gas and dust increased. This was due to conservation of angular momentum. That's the physics principle behind a spinning ice skater pulling in their arms, making them spin faster. There was hardly any rotation in the giant cloud at first, but as it got smaller, it was like pulling in the arms of the whole thing.

A newly formed planetary system

The rotation and the gravitational force caused most of the material to flatten out. What was essentially a fuzzy blob turned into a relatively flat disk. It's kind of like how spinning a ball of pizza dough will make it flatten into a disk shape.

Our biggest planets formed in a similar way to how the entire solar system formed. The smaller planets started as many small pieces of material that occasionally ran into one another and stuck together to form larger objects. This process, called *accretion*, occurred over long periods of time.

FUN FACT

By human standards, the solar system is huge. The *Voyager 2* spacecraft traveled tens of thousands of miles per hour and still took 12 years to reach the farthest planet, Neptune. At those speeds, it would take tens of thousands of years to reach another "close" star. What about the size of our galaxy? Think of it this way: If the part of the solar system between the Sun and Neptune were the size of a U.S. quarter, the Milky Way galaxy would be about the size of the continent of North America!

SPACE FUNDAMENTALS

Planetary science is the study of planets and the solar system. This overlaps with the more recognizable term **astronomy**, which is the study of anything in space, typically using telescopes. In addition to astronomy, planetary science involves aspects of a number of different sciences, including physics, chemistry, geology, and even biology.

The following sections cover the fundamentals of planetary science. We will look at the basic structure of the solar system, gravity and orbits, and the surprisingly complex question of how we define a planet. We'll also explore how people are able to learn what planets and stars are made of when we're so far away from them. Before we get into all of this, it helps to understand how planetary scientists talk about distance over such large areas of space.

MEASUREMENTS IN SPACE

Earth is about 93 million miles (150 million kilometers) from the Sun. The distance from Neptune is about thirty times greater. Planetary scientists got tired of using such giant numbers all the time, so they frequently use the **astronomical unit (AU)**. One AU is the average distance between the Earth and the Sun. It's an average because Earth gets somewhat closer and farther from the Sun during its orbit. How far is Neptune from the Sun? Instead of a long number in the billions, all we have to say is about 30 AU. You'll see this abbreviation throughout the book.

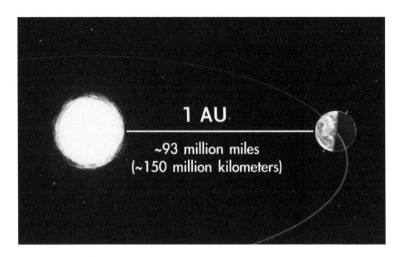

1 AU

~93 million miles
(~150 million kilometers)

WHAT IS A PLANET?

The word *planet* derives from a Greek word meaning "wanderer." The pattern of stars we see in the sky is always the same, but ancient Greeks noticed five bright, starlike objects that wandered through the field of stars from night to night, week to week. These five objects were called planets: Mercury, Venus, Mars, Jupiter, and Saturn.

Before the invention of telescopes, the definition of a planet included only the five wandering objects that were easy to see with your eyes. But after the telescope was introduced in the early 1600s, more and more objects were discovered throughout the solar system. The way we define a planet has evolved and changed over time. The current definition from the International Astronomical Union has three criteria.

First, a planet has to move in a path around the Sun—not another body. Objects that **orbit** another body are called moons or **natural satellites**. Second, a planet must be big enough that its own gravity forms the body into a round or spherical shape. Finally, a planet must have cleared the neighborhood around its orbit. Basically, this means there is nothing of similar size and a similar orbit around the Sun.

Earth, the Moon, and Pluto to scale

The first two requirements also apply to dwarf planets, a category that was first defined in 2006. Ceres was called a planet long ago; then it was called an asteroid. It is now considered a dwarf planet because it has a similar orbit to other nearby objects. Similarly, Pluto was reclassified from a planet to a dwarf planet because of the numerous trans-Neptunian objects in its region.

CAREERS IN ASTRONOMY

Scientists who study our solar system ask lots of questions to learn more about it—what is in it, how does it currently work, and how has it evolved. They try to answer these questions through their work and research. They may use experimental data from a laboratory, from a telescope, or from spacecraft. They may also do theoretical studies, where equations and computers are used to make models of planetary **phenomena** to understand them better.

There are many ways to become a scientist, but it all starts with a well-rounded education. This involves studying math and science in high school and college in addition to developing writing and thinking skills. After undergraduate college, almost all scientists go on to get a PhD in their field of specialty. This is a degree where you conduct original research as well as classroom study. There are lots of different careers in astronomy with different schooling requirements. Look out for the Careers in Astronomy sections in this book to find out more.

SOLAR SYSTEM STRUCTURE

The Sun is at the center of the solar system, and everything revolves around it, including eight planets. The four closest planets to the Sun are called **terrestrial planets** or **rocky planets**. They are Mercury, Venus, Earth, and Mars. They all have rocky surfaces that you could imagine standing on. These planets have varying amounts of **atmosphere**, the gas surrounding the planet. Mercury and Venus don't have a moon, whereas Earth has one and Mars has two.

Much farther out are the **giant planets**: Jupiter, Saturn, Uranus, and Neptune. All are enormous compared to Earth, and they are mostly made of **gas**. They have no solid surface to stand on. All have many moons.

Planets in order from the Sun, shown to scale

There are billions of other smaller objects in the solar system. Rocky asteroids are mostly in the asteroid belt between Mars and Jupiter. But other asteroids are scattered throughout the solar system. Thousands of icy objects have been discovered beyond the orbit of Neptune, including Pluto and Eris. Comets are like big dirty snowballs that head toward the Sun periodically. When they're warmed by sunlight, they give off gas, ice, and dust—this forms the bright tails they are so famous for.

GRAVITY AND ORBITS

Gravity is the force that holds our solar system together. In the 1600s, English physicist Isaac Newton figured out the law of gravitational force. This equation explains why objects fall on the Earth and how the planets move around the Sun. Newton showed that gravitational force was proportional to mass. Basically, things with more mass have more gravity. That is why big, massive objects like the Earth and the Sun exert strong gravitational force.

So if the Sun has so much gravity, why doesn't the Earth get pulled into it? Because the Earth is moving very fast. This motion balances out the gravity pulling toward the Sun.

An orbit is the path an object follows around another object—like how Earth moves around the Sun. Orbits are determined by that balance between orbital speed and gravity. All the planets orbit in an oval-like shape called an **ellipse**.

Illustration of an elliptical orbit

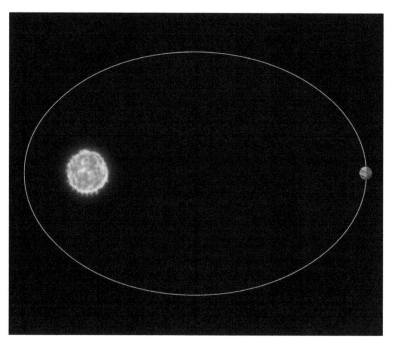

ELECTROMAGNETIC SPECTRUM

The **electromagnetic spectrum** is the entire range of light that exists. What we can see with our eyes, known as visible light, is just a small portion of this broad spectrum. All light is made up of waves. The shorter wavelengths of visible light are blue and violet. The next shorter wavelengths are ultraviolet (UV) light. We can't see this light, but we can sometimes feel its effects in our everyday life—ultraviolet is what causes sunburn on your skin. Beyond the ultraviolet are X-rays and gamma rays. Infrared, microwaves, and radio waves are all longer wavelengths.

What does all this have to do with the solar system? Well, an important method to study planets, stars, and other objects is to use scientific instruments that allow us to "see" the many different parts of the electromagnetic spectrum. In this book, you'll come across images and data representing many wavelengths.

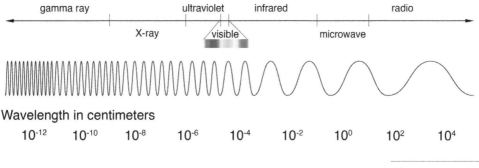

Wavelength in centimeters

10^{-12} 10^{-10} 10^{-8} 10^{-6} 10^{-4} 10^{-2} 10^{0} 10^{2} 10^{4}

The electromagnetic spectrum

Studying the "color" of something such as the surface of a planet can tell us what materials that surface is made of. We use telescopic observations at various wavelengths to do this more precisely. Sometimes we can use visible colors of things to get an idea of what they're made of: leaves are often green, tree trunks brown, and golden retrievers are often "golden." This study of the electromagnetic spectrum is called **spectroscopy**.

THE SUN

The Sun is by far the closest star to Earth. The next closest star is over four light-years away. That is why the Sun appears as a disk in the sky, whereas other stars appear as dots of light.

Sunlight allows liquid water to stabilize on Earth's surface. This is important because liquid water is required by all life on Earth. In a nutshell, we wouldn't be here without the Sun. It's also the energy

The Sun over Earth's horizon

source that drives weather, climate, and ocean currents.

The Sun is sometimes classified as a yellow **dwarf star**, although this name is a little misleading. Despite the impression we get from sunsets and from art, the Sun is not yellow, orange, or red. It's actually white. Our atmosphere scatters blue light from the visible spectrum, which leaves that yellow-orange color when we see the Sun in the sky. Reminder: Never look directly at the Sun. It could fry your eyes—okay, perhaps not literally, but it could damage them!

Our Sun has been here for around five billion years and will be here doing its thing for another five billion years or more. After that time, it will eventually reach the final stages of its normal life. The outer layers will expand beyond the orbit of Venus, the second-closest planet to the Sun, and toast Earth in the process. It will be what is called a **red giant**. Then it will collapse into a remnant of a star known as a **white dwarf**. But don't worry: There's plenty of Sun fun between now and then.

THE STRUCTURE OF THE SUN

The Sun is truly enormous. It's so huge that you could fit 1.3 million Earths inside the Sun.

The Sun's mass is about 75 percent hydrogen and about 25 percent helium, with small amounts of other elements. The material in the

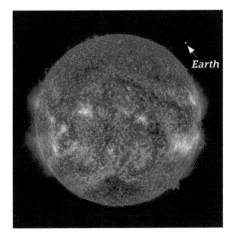

The Sun with Earth for scale

Sun is **plasma**. Plasma is a state of matter, along with solids, liquids, and gases. You know how when you boil liquid it can change to gas? Similarly, heating a gas will form plasma. A plasma is like a gas in many ways—they both lack a distinct shape or volume. But plasma is composed of positively charged particles and negatively charged particles, whereas gas has only neutral particles. Plasmas tend to occur in extremely high-temperature environments.

All the pressure within the Sun causes something called **nuclear fusion**. This is why the Sun is hot. Nuclear fusion converts a small amount of the mass of the hydrogen atoms into energy while converting the rest into helium. The energy released from this process is huge. That process is going on all the time in the core of the Sun. Energy escapes through the large, layered Sun to reach where we see it in the form of light.

THE CORE, THE RADIATIVE ZONE, AND THE CONVECTIVE ZONE

Layers of the Sun's interior

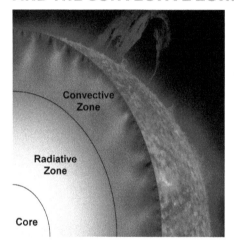

Convective Zone

Radiative Zone

Core

The inner portion of the Sun is called the **core**. That's where nuclear fusion occurs and where energy is produced. The temperature at the center of the Sun is about 27 million degrees Fahrenheit (15 million degrees Celsius). The density of the material there is about 160 times the density of water, or more than 13 times the density of lead.

All the energy produced from nuclear fusion tries to make its way out of the gigantic Sun. Particles of light called **photons** are released in this process and carry energy. The radiative zone is the layer around the Sun's core. It gets its name from the way energy is carried through this layer. Electromagnetic radiation in the form of photons carries most of the energy.

Moving out from the radiative zone, we reach the convective zone. The densities become lower in this final layer of the Sun's interior. Hotter material down below is able to rise because of its lower density. This is called **convection**. It's the same basic principle behind hot-air balloons—air inside the balloon is heated and becomes less dense, causing it to rise above the surrounding colder air. In the Sun, hotter material rises until it reaches the surface.

THE PHOTOSPHERE, THE CHROMOSPHERE, AND THE CORONA

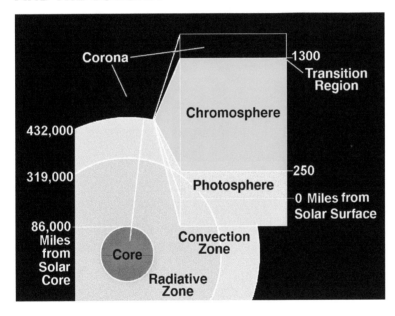

Layers of the Sun

The photosphere is what we see from Earth. It is where visible light, as well as other wavelengths of light, is able to escape from the Sun without running into something. It is what we might think of as the "surface" of the Sun, but it's really more like the first layer of the Sun's atmosphere.

Above the photosphere is the chromosphere. This is a layer of thinner plasma that is not visible from Earth, except during solar eclipses. When the Moon is in front of the Sun during an eclipse, the chromosphere forms a somewhat colorful band around the Moon. That is how the chromosphere gets its name—*chromo* is derived from the Greek word for color. Temperatures in this region of the Sun rise to tens of thousands of degrees.

Chromosphere and corona during an eclipse

The chromosphere transitions to the corona. The word *corona* means "crown," which is sort of what this part of the Sun looks like during a total solar eclipse. The corona is much less dense, so it has fewer particles. But it is much hotter than the photosphere or chromosphere, reaching temperatures of millions of degrees.

THE "SURFACE" OF THE SUN

To learn more about the "surface" of the Sun, let's go back to the photosphere. Earth is mostly affected by this layer, the layers above it, and the material that flows out from them. The photosphere's temperature is about 10,000 degrees Fahrenheit (5,530 degrees Celsius). This is the temperature that naturally emits light in the visible part of the electromagnetic spectrum. Humans and other animals on Earth evolved to see the strongest wavelengths of light emitted by the Sun. That is why the visible part of the spectrum is, well, visible!

The Sun is white, representing a fairly even distribution of light across the rainbow of colors in the visible spectrum. Hotter stars put out more light in the ultraviolet and blue parts of the spectrum. Cooler stars put out more light in the red and infrared. Thus, our eyes see hotter stars as blue and cooler stars as red.

Blue (hotter) and red (cooler) stars

Light from the Sun reaches the Earth in about eight minutes. That means the Sun we see from Earth is actually the Sun as it was eight minutes ago. Mind-bending, right? Besides light, the Sun also spits out bursts of charged particles. They reach the Earth in a couple of days and can even wreak havoc with satellites and power grids.

The Sun in UV light. Loops seen here are charged particles following the magnetic field.

We can see a lot of interesting solar phenomena with proper safety filters from the surface of the Earth. Even more phenomena are visible from spacecraft that observe in shorter wavelengths, such as ultraviolet and X-ray. Some of these wavelengths get blocked by the Earth's atmosphere, so you can see them only in space above. People tend to think of the Sun as something constant—it rises every morning, sets every evening, and provides sunlight every day. In that respect, it's pretty constant. But there are all sorts of active, amazing phenomena occurring on the Sun on a regular basis.

MAGNETOSPHERES, SOLAR WIND, AND AURORA

The movement of electrically charged particles generates magnetic fields. A magnetic field is the region around a magnet. Think of a refrigerator magnet: When you go to stick it on your refrigerator, you'll feel a point where it starts to pull and then stick to the refrigerator surface. This magnet's field is small and exerts significant force only within a few inches. The magnetic field of the Earth, however, is large. It affects a big region of space and causes compasses to point toward magnetic north. Metals moving inside the Earth generate Earth's magnetic field. The movement of charged particles in the Sun's plasma generates a lot of complex magnetic fields. The region of a planetary body or a star affected by its magnetic field is called the **magnetosphere**.

There is a constant high-speed flow of electrically charged particles coming out from the Sun. We call this the **solar wind**. It generates magnetic fields and effectively extends the Sun's magnetic field out past Neptune, the farthest planet in the solar system.

When charged particles hit the Earth's magnetosphere, some of the particles are directed along the magnetic field to our planet's magnetic poles. When these particles interact with the upper atmosphere, it causes a release of light. This creates the spectacular phenomena we see from Earth called the northern and southern lights, also known as the Aurora Borealis and Aurora Australis.

Aurora Borealis, the northern lights

SUNSPOTS, SOLAR FLARES, PROMINENCES, AND CORONAL MASS EJECTIONS

The Sun often has dark spots on it called **sunspots**. They result from localized temporary changes in the magnetic field. The spots are not actually dark—they're just cooler, which means they put out less light than the surrounding Sun.

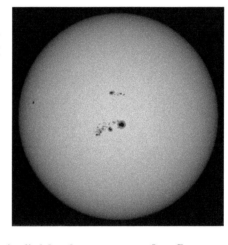

Sunspots in visible light

Changes in magnetic fields also cause **solar flares**. This is the intense brightening of a specific area on the Sun. A solar flare gives off a burst of bright light, including high-energy X-rays. Sometimes these flares are also associated with prominences, which are enormous features that extend out from the Sun. A solar prominence is plasma that reaches up from the photosphere all the way into the corona.

Solar flare at different UV wavelengths

Solar activity, including sunspots and solar flares, reaches a peak about every eleven years.

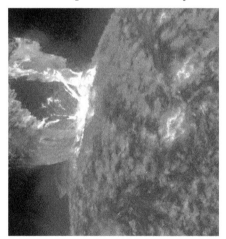

Solar prominence produces a coronal mass ejection

During these times of high solar activity, coronal mass ejections (CMEs) may occur. CMEs are huge ejections of charged particles, sort of a solar windstorm. If Earth is along the path of a CME, the increased particles will cause those light displays called auroras. CMEs can also cause damage to satellites and even affect power grids on Earth. The largest known storm to hit Earth was in 1859, causing multiple telegraph systems to spark and even catch fire. In 1989, a CME knocked out power in Quebec, Canada, for many hours.

One of the biggest unsolved mysteries is why the corona, the outer atmosphere of the Sun, is so hot. It is millions of degrees. The temperature of the layers below the corona—the photosphere and the chromosphere—are only thousands of degrees. Normally, when something gets farther from a heat source, it gets cooler. For example, the closer you stand to a fire, the warmer you'll get. But with the corona, the farther it is from the surface of the Sun, the hotter it gets. And not just hotter, but *much* hotter.

There are many theories to try to explain this, but there is no agreement on which theory is right. Almost all theories involve magnetic fields and the movement of plasma transporting energy to the corona. Like many scientific theories about our solar system, the details are still being worked out.

SOLAR ECLIPSES

A solar eclipse occurs when the Moon passes in front of the Sun. There are two types of solar eclipse. A partial eclipse happens when part of the Sun is covered. A total eclipse happens when the entire Sun gets covered for a few minutes and they often occur a couple of times per year, but they aren't always easy to see. Total eclipses can be seen from only a small part of the Earth, and the location is different almost every time. People often travel very far to see one.

The part of a total solar eclipse with full Sun coverage is called totality. When this happens, the sky becomes dark except at the horizon. Partial solar eclipses are more common. This is mostly because the path of any total solar eclipse has a wide region of partial eclipse alongside it.

Total solar eclipse

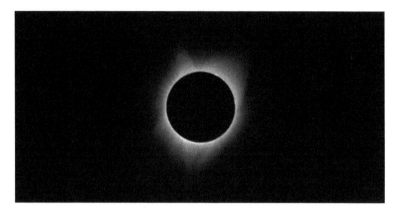

Total solar eclipses are one of the most amazing astronomical phenomena that you can observe. But don't look at the Sun, except during totality. You could cause major damage to your eyes. Instead, use proper solar filter glasses (not sunglasses!) or a pinhole in a piece of cardboard. This projects an image of the

Eclipse viewed through a pinhole

eclipse onto a piece of paper. The Earth and the Moon orbits are extremely well known, so eclipses can be very accurately predicted. Check out the Resources section at the back of this book to see how you can find information on upcoming solar eclipses.

The inner planets

TWO

TERRESTRIAL PLANETS AND ASTEROIDS

The inner solar system has the four planets closest to the Sun: Mercury, Venus, Earth, and Mars. We call them many names, including terrestrial planets, the inner planets, rocky planets, and Earthlike planets. Except for Earth, they are all very hostile places with harsh conditions that make them unlivable for humans and most forms of life. Their smaller size, shorter orbits, and solid surfaces make them different from the outer planets.

Asteroids are also part of the inner solar system. They are relatively small rocky objects that lie mostly between the orbit of Mars and Jupiter. This region is called the asteroid belt. Other asteroids come closer to Earth and Earth's orbit.

MERCURY

DIAMETER: *3,032 miles (4,879 kilometers)*

MASS: *0.06 Earth masses*

AVERAGE DISTANCE FROM THE SUN: *0.39 AU*

KNOWN MOONS: *0*

LENGTH OF DAY: *176 Earth days (4,223 hours)*

LENGTH OF YEAR: *0.24 Earth years (88 days)*

AVERAGE TEMPERATURE: *333 degrees Fahrenheit (167 degrees Celsius)*

Mercury (MUR-kyer-ee) is the closest planet to the Sun. It is also the smallest planet. If Mercury were the size of a softball, the Earth would be about the size of a basketball. From Earth, Mercury looks like a fairly bright star. Because we're able to see it easily with our eyes, it has been known since ancient times.

Mercury

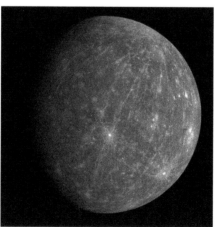

Mercury is the fastest-moving planet. This causes it to move more rapidly than others in the night sky as seen from Earth. It's also why the Romans named this planet after their speedy messenger god, Mercury. Because of this speed, Mercury is one of the hardest planets for us to reach. Few spacecraft have explored Mercury.

Mariner 10 was the first spacecraft sent to study the planet. It flew by in the 1970s but was only able to photograph a little over half the planet. It was not until 2008, when the *MESSENGER* spacecraft flew by and later orbited, that we had a complete picture of the planet.

MERCURY'S ATMOSPHERE

Mercury has almost no atmosphere. It is essentially a **vacuum** on the planet's surface. This means there is nothing to protect it from the impacts of small and large particles traveling at high speeds. It also means there is no protection from the solar wind, charged particles bombarding the surface, or ultraviolet and other electromagnetic radiation.

Technically, it does have the *tiniest* bit of atmosphere. This is partly from particles that have been knocked off the planet's surface by the solar wind. But this "atmosphere"

Infrared views of Mercury's surface

is incredibly thin, what is known as an **exosphere**. Earth has an exosphere, but it begins 300 miles (500 kilometers) above the surface. That's far beyond where we consider space to begin. Mercury's atmosphere is all exosphere. It begins at Mercury's surface.

MERCURY'S SURFACE

Lacking any significant atmosphere, much less liquid water, Mercury hasn't experienced much erosion. Wind, water, and ice cause erosion on Earth and shape our natural landscape. Our world has also been shaped by **plate tectonics**, activity under the surface that causes things such as volcanoes and earthquakes. Mercury's absence of plate tectonics and erosion has allowed its surface to preserve a record of the early solar system. Like the Moon, Mercury is covered in impact craters of all sizes. There were many more rocks flying around early in the solar system. Eventually these rocks got swept up, mostly by planets and other large bodies.

Impact craters on Mercury

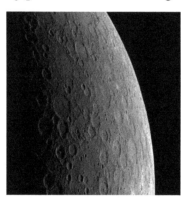

Smaller impact craters are bowl shaped. Larger impacts cause larger structures with flat floors, mountains, and even rings. Mercury has one of the largest impact basins in the solar system, the Caloris (ka-LOR-iss) Basin, with a diameter of 960 miles (1,550 kilometers).

Caloris Basin (circular orange feature)

Mercury runs hot and cold. Because of its proximity to the Sun, Mercury's surface reaches 800 degrees Fahrenheit (430 degrees Celsius). Because it has no atmosphere to serve as a blanket at night and because nights are 88 Earth days long, the surface will drop as low as −290 degrees Fahrenheit (−180 degrees Celsius).

A **solar day** is 24 hours for Earth. It is one complete day-to-night cycle. Mercury has a solar day that lasts about 176 Earth days. It takes 88 days to orbit the Sun. That means one day on Mercury is about two times longer than its year (one orbit around the Sun). If you were on Mercury, one Mercurian day would take two Mercurian years!

On a related note, one complete rotation of a planet relative to the stars is called a **sidereal day**. For Earth, the sidereal day and solar day are different by only four minutes. For Mercury, the differences are huge. Mercury has three sidereal days (each about 58.7 Earth days) for every two Mercurian years.

MERCURY'S STRUCTURE

Mercury has a unique internal structure among the planets. It is thought to have two main layers: an outer shell and a metallic core. What is different about Mercury is the core is a much larger percentage of the planet than elsewhere in the solar system. Its core takes up 85 percent of the diameter of the planet, compared to 54 percent for Earth. Different theories are being examined to explain this. One theory suggests a different composition of the inner part of the nebula that formed our solar system. Another theory is an impact of a nearly planet-size object more than four billion years ago, which could have stripped off

Mercury's outer layers. Because of its large metal core, Mercury is the second densest planet after Earth.

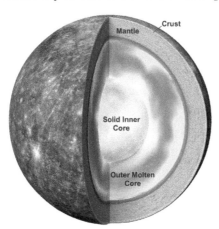

Mercury's interior structure

Mercury has a lot of iron and other metals, similar to what moves in the Earth and generates our magnetic field. Because Mercury is much smaller than Earth, scientists assumed the interior had cooled much more than the Earth's. They thought that would freeze the core, preventing any motion and the possibility of a magnetic field. But in 1974, scientists were surprised to find that Mercury has an active magnetic field. Tidal effects tied to its orbit may keep some of the core molten.

NOTEWORTHY FEATURES

On Mercury, there is water ice at the bottom of craters near the poles. How does the same planet that reaches 800 degrees Fahrenheit (430 degrees Celsius) have frozen ice at its poles? There are places in shadowed craters that never see sunlight. In addition to this, there is essentially no atmosphere to transport heat. The dusty, fluffy surface is poor at transmitting heat, too. All this means the water ice just stays there. A similar process occurs on the Moon.

As Mercury cooled from the intense heat when the planet first formed, the outer crust shrank. This caused mountains to rise as a result. These are called

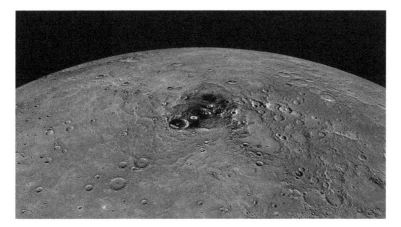

Water ice locations (shown in yellow)

wrinkle ridges. It's similar to what would happen if you took a frosted cake and squished it from the sides.

Some craters on Mercury have white-colored areas with pits in them. These are called hollows. They were first discovered in images taken by the *MESSENGER* spacecraft in 2011. Scientists had never seen anything like them before in the solar system. It is believed they are formed in a process where material turns from a solid directly into a gas, leaving holes.

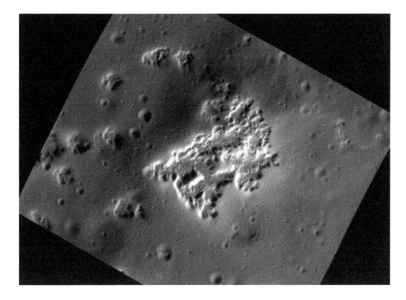

Hollows on Mercury

KEY FIGURES IN HISTORY

Galileo Galilei

GALILEO GALILEI *(1564–1642)* made the first telescopic observations of Mercury. He built one of the first telescopes and was the first person to use one to study the night sky. Among other things, he discovered that Venus had phases just like our Moon. The phases are the different ways these objects look from Earth—for example, the crescent moon and the quarter moon.

One of Galileo's most significant discoveries was the four largest moons of Jupiter, now known as the Galilean satellites. He realized these were objects orbiting around Jupiter. At the time, the prevailing thought was that everything revolved around the Earth. Galileo reported his observations and supported the theory of Polish astronomer Copernicus: Earth and other planets revolve around the Sun. For his efforts, Galileo was put under house arrest for the rest of his life by the Catholic Church. During that time, the Copernican theory was viewed as something that went against the beliefs of the Church.

FACT SHEET

VENUS

DIAMETER: *7,521 miles (12,104 kilometers)*

MASS: *0.82 Earth masses*

AVERAGE DISTANCE FROM THE SUN: *0.73 AU*

KNOWN MOONS: *0*

LENGTH OF DAY: *243 Earth days (5,832 hours)*

LENGTH OF YEAR: *0.615 Earth years (224.7 days)*

AVERAGE TEMPERATURE: *867 degrees Fahrenheit (464 degrees Celsius)*

Venus (VEE-nuhs) is the second planet from the Sun. It is sometimes called Earth's sister planet because it's similar in size. Venus has the hottest surface temperatures in the solar system. The planet also has sulfuric acid rain and a crushing atmosphere.

Besides the Moon, Venus is the brightest natural object in the night sky. It looks like an extremely bright star. As such, it's been known since ancient times. It is named after the Roman goddess of love and beauty.

Mariner 10 *image of Venus*

Radar mosaic of Venus

The planet rotates very slowly. One day on Venus lasts about 243 Earth days. It also rotates retrograde, meaning the opposite direction from Earth and the other planets in the solar system. The Sun rises in the west and sets in the east.

We can't see the surface of Venus from space because clouds obscure the view. But spacecraft have visited and used radar that can "see" through the clouds to the surface.

VENUS'S ATMOSPHERE

The atmosphere of Venus is brutal. The surface of Venus has crushing pressures. It has about ninety times the surface pressure of Earth, equivalent to 3,000 feet (1 kilometer) under Earth's ocean. And

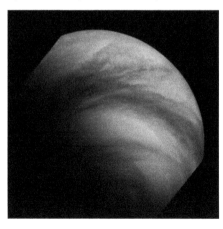

Clouds over Venus

that's not the only brutal thing—opaque clouds of sulfuric acid surround the planet.

There is almost no wind at the surface, but there are extremely fast winds higher in the atmosphere. This includes the wind that blows clouds all the way around the planet in about four Earth days. The speeds are equivalent to Earth's strongest hurricane winds.

Venus's atmosphere is about 95 percent carbon dioxide. That's the stuff that makes bubbles in carbonated drinks like soda, but it's also a greenhouse gas. You might have heard about Earth's rising temperatures due to the increase of greenhouse gases. But what exactly is the greenhouse effect?

Visible light that carries most of the energy from the Sun can pass through the carbon dioxide easily. It then gets absorbed by the atmosphere and by the surface. The surface and atmosphere give off infrared light based upon their temperature. On planets other than Venus, most of the infrared light, basically heat, can escape fairly easily. But carbon dioxide absorbs those wavelengths of light. That makes it harder for heat to escape. The result is a greenhouse effect, causing the hottest surface temperatures in the solar system—almost 900 degrees Fahrenheit (482 degrees Celsius), which is hot enough to melt lead.

VENUS'S SURFACE

Venus has a complex geological surface with a variety of features, from mountains to plains to lava channels to impact craters. In contrast to Mercury or the Moon, whose surfaces in some places are four billion years old, Venus has a young surface. We know this because of the relatively few craters on its surface. The number of craters we see indicates ages of several hundred million years nearly everywhere. That implies Venus was almost completely resurfaced several hundred million years ago.

Surface of Venus from Soviet spacecraft, Venera 13

Most of Venus's surface, about 80 percent, is covered with volcanic plains. There are two areas of highlands: Ishtar Terra in the north and Aphrodite Terra near the equator. These areas are sort of like continents on Earth. Venus is relatively flat, but the two highland regions are exceptions. The highest mountain on the planet, Maxwell Montes, is about 36,000 feet (11 kilometers) above Venus's average surface elevation. For comparison, Mount Everest is about 29,000 feet (8.8 kilometers) above sea level.

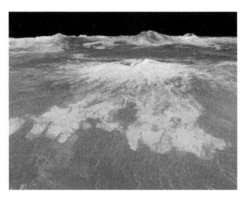

Volcanoes and other features on Venus

Venus has more volcanoes than any other planet in the solar system. Although some studies suggest some might have erupted in the geologically recent past, none are known to be active. There are at least 1,500 volcanoes and volcanic features that have been identified. There could be millions more!

Venus has been explored not only with flyby spacecraft, but also with balloons! Besides Earth, Venus is the only terrestrial planet with a thick atmosphere that allows balloons to work effectively. The Soviet Union's space program deployed 12-foot-diameter balloons *Vega 1* and *Vega 2* in the 1980s. They stayed about 34 miles (54 kilometers) above the scorching-hot surface in a region where temperatures were mild. They were dropped on the side of the planet where it was nighttime and then blown by the strong winds onto the day side. Both *Vega* balloons and their scientific equipment operated for more than 46 hours before their batteries died.

VENUS'S STRUCTURE

Venus is almost as large as Earth, which is why it's thought to have a similar internal structure: a metallic core at its center, a thick layer called a mantle, and a rocky crust as the surface layer. But unlike Earth, Venus lacks an internally driven magnetic field. This might be due to

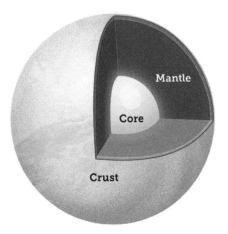

Venus's interior structure

less convection or other motion of material inside the planet.

Although the interior of Venus doesn't generate a magnetic field, the planet does have a very weak magnetic field caused by two effects of the Sun. Ultraviolet light interacts with the upper parts of Venus's atmosphere and breaks apart the molecules, creating charged particles. Along comes the strong solar wind with its own magnetic field. The solar wind's magnetic field causes the charged particles in the upper atmosphere to move. Because those charged particles are moving, they generate their own magnetic field.

NOTEWORTHY FEATURES

Venus's pancake domes

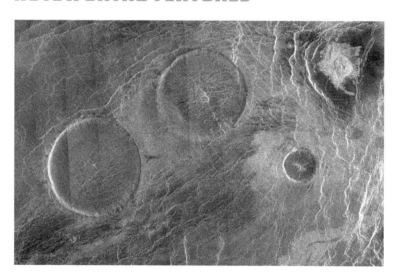

Pancake domes might sound like something you eat for breakfast, but they're actually a unique type of structure seen on Venus. These circular, relatively flat domes of lava are nearly perfect circles. They appear to have been made from gooey lava coming out from a single location, which then spread out under the

enormous pressure of the atmosphere. This flatten-
ing process formed the pancake-like shapes. They
are somewhat like volcanic features seen beneath the
Earth's ocean.

Another type of volcanic feature seen on Venus is
coronae. They are often several hundred miles across
and look vaguely like crowns. They are huge circular
features that may have formed from magma, a molten
material that becomes lava when it cools. When
magma pushes up from the mantle, it can create a
round dome on the planet's surface. Then the dome
could have collapsed in the center and leaked out lava.

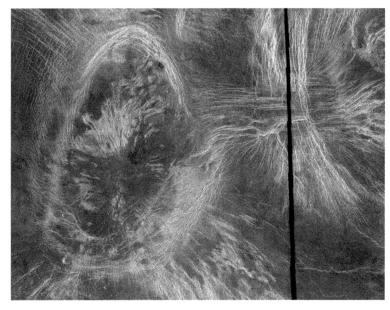

*Two Venus
coronae:
Bahet Corona
and Onatah
Corona*

The longest channel in the solar system is on
Venus. Called Baltis Vallis (BALL-tiss VAL-iss), it
formed not by water flow but by lava flow. It is about
4,200 miles (6,800 kilometers) long, making it a
little longer than the Nile River of Africa. The lava
would have flowed quite freely, more similar to water
than to mud.

SPACE IN DAILY LIFE

If you've ever used the camera on a cell phone, you've used technology from NASA and the space program. NASA relies on quality imaging in its spacecraft to bring clear pictures back from space. But spacecraft have severe limitations on size and power, so NASA is interested in making spacecraft instruments as small and as low-powered as possible.

In 1990, Eric Fossum at NASA's Jet Propulsion Laboratory was hired to work on these topics. At the time, charge-coupled devices, or CCDs, dominated as image sensors, but they required significant power. (CCDs are used in digital cameras, photocopiers, and other devices.) In 1993, Fossum invented something called a CMOS image sensor. The same things that make CMOS image sensors ideal for spacecraft are what make them ideal for phone cameras: They're small and use little power, even with large images or video. The next time you take a selfie, thank the space program!

EARTH

DIAMETER: *7,926 miles (12,756 kilometers)*

MASS: *1 Earth mass*

AVERAGE DISTANCE FROM THE SUN: *1 AU*

KNOWN MOONS: *1*

LENGTH OF DAY: *1 Earth day (24 hours)*

LENGTH OF YEAR: *1 Earth year (365.25 days)*

AVERAGE TEMPERATURE: *59 degrees Fahrenheit (15 degrees Celsius)*

Earth is the largest of the terrestrial planets and the third planet from the Sun.

Earth is in the habitable zone of our solar system. This is the region around a star where it's not too hot or too cold for liquid water to exist

Earth as seen from the Moon

on the surface of a planet. Liquid water is one of the few things required by all life on Earth. So far, Earth is the only place in the universe where we know life exists. Life even affects the planet, from changing its atmosphere to changing the landscape.

The Earth's rotation is what causes our twenty-four-hour day. Earth's rotation is much faster than Mercury's and Venus's and is similar to Mars's. Our orbit is nearly

North and South America seen from space

circular, so our distance from the Sun does not change much over the course of a year. That means the heat we get from the Sun doesn't change much either. Our different seasons are driven by the way the planet tilts as it rotates around its **axis**.

EARTH'S ATMOSPHERE

The atmosphere is crucial to all life on Earth. It is about 78 percent nitrogen, 21 percent oxygen, and smaller amounts of other gases. Amazingly, the presence of oxygen in the atmosphere is primarily due to the actions of plants over billions of years.

Antarctica and southern Africa

Long-term and short-term wind patterns are active within the atmosphere. Our clouds are composed of water, which precipitates in the form of liquid water (rain) or solid water (snow).

Our atmosphere protects life from the

Sun's harmful radiation. This includes forms of light such as X-rays, gamma rays, and high-energy ultraviolet, absorbed in part by a layer of ozone gas high in the atmosphere.

Minor parts of the atmosphere, such as carbon dioxide, methane, and water, act as greenhouse gases. These gases allow the easy passing of visible light

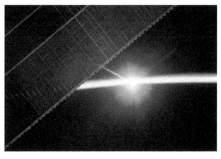

Sunrise from the International Space Station

from the Sun, but they also absorb some infrared light emitted by the surface and atmosphere. This creates a warming of the atmosphere and surface. Venus also has a greenhouse effect, but Earth's is much smaller because there are much smaller amounts of carbon dioxide in its atmosphere. There has been an increase in greenhouse gases since the beginning of the Industrial Revolution a few hundred years ago, which has caused the global temperature to rise.

EARTH'S SURFACE

There are at least three major things that make Earth's surface unique in the solar system: large quantities of liquid water, life, and large-scale plate tectonics.

New Zealand, ocean, and clouds from space

Water covers over two-thirds of our planet. It also creates much faster erosion than we see in the present day on other planets.

Life has the capability to resurface the land, change the flow of water, and even affect the climate.

The theory of plate tectonics explains so much of our large-scale geological activity, such as the formation of continents and mountains. Although it might seem obvious in hindsight, it took a long time for scientists to come up with this theory. The idea was developed during the first half of the 1900s and was not fully accepted until the 1960s. What scientists realized is that the Earth's outer layer is made of giant chunks. These chunks are known as plates. They fit together like puzzle pieces and move along a gooey layer below the surface. This movement happens slowly over time. At plate boundaries, there tend to be a lot of earthquakes and volcanoes. They can sometimes cause material to be cycled downward on the edge of a plate. When this occurs, new material comes out from somewhere else to take its place. All of this results in very active geology that continues to reshape and form Earth's surface.

Earth's fifteen largest plates

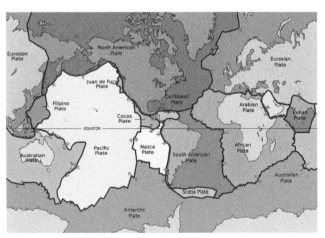

The International Space Station is a large spacecraft that orbits Earth from an altitude of 250 miles (400 kilometers). Communications satellites and TV satellites reach orbits about 100 times higher at 25,000 miles (40,000 kilometers) altitude. They have to go up that high to remain over the same location on the surface of the Earth. Their orbit has a period that matches the Earth's rotation. The Moon is about 1,000 times farther than the International Space Station's altitude, about 250,000 miles (400,000 kilometers).

International Space Station

EARTH'S STRUCTURE

Earth has the highest average density in the solar system. This is thanks to the planet's rocky outer layers of crust and mantle and the metallic iron and nickel of the inner and outer cores. The stuff down deep gets squished to a higher density by all the stuff above it. You might think Mercury's incredibly large metallic core in relation to its size would make it the densest planet. You might even think the largest planets would have the most density because of their sheer size. But Earth is still the densest object in our solar system.

How do we know what's inside a planet? On Earth, we have many ways to find out. We can drill holes near the surface. The material coming out from volcanoes gives us an idea of the upper portions of the Earth. Seismic studies, the studies of earthquakes, tell us a great deal of information about the interior.

Earth's interior structure

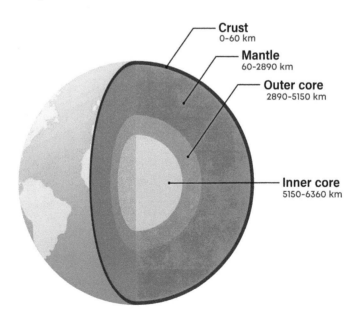

Crust
0-60 km

Mantle
60-2890 km

Outer core
2890-5150 km

Inner core
5150-6360 km

The gravity experienced by a flying spacecraft changes depending on the density distribution of materials inside a planet. Another method is assessing details of a planetary body's rotation, looking for small variations that will relate to differences in the interior.

NOTEWORTHY FEATURES

From the Grand Canyon to Mount Everest and beyond, there are more noteworthy features on Earth than we can even begin to cover here. You're probably familiar with a lot of them, so let's look at what's missing from our planetary surface: lots of impact craters.

There are impact craters preserved on the Earth's surface, but only a few hundred. Many of those are barely recogniz-able as anything other than

Meteor crater in Arizona

vague circular features. So what does this tell us? In the early days of the solar system, objects slammed into other objects frequently. Fortunately for us, that happens less often now. This is because most of the objects have already run into each other over the 4.5-billion-year history of the solar system. But impacts still happen, so if we don't see impact craters, it means the surface is comparatively young.

Water erosion, weathering from the atmosphere, and the recycling of materials by plate tectonics have removed traces of impact craters on Earth. This is unlike most other planetary bodies. But there are a couple of exceptions, including the planet Venus and Io, a moon of Jupiter that has active volcanoes.

CAREERS IN ASTRONOMY

Engineers play crucial roles in space exploration and astronomy. They design and build all the technology, instruments, and machines that are used in those fields. Those includes spacecraft, rockets, telescopes, and scientific equipment. Their job is to turn ideas into reality. They design and frequently operate what scientists need to explore space and conduct their research. Many fields of engineering are involved in space-related topics. Aerospace engineers design rockets and spacecraft. Components are designed by electrical engineers and mechanical engineers. Computer systems are overseen by system engineers. The list goes on.

Engineering relies on math and science to create things. Pursuing an engineering career means taking math, science, and, of course, specialized engineering courses in college. Engineers in the aerospace field typically need a master's degree, though entry-level positions are available for people who hold bachelor's degrees. Engineers in academia, as well as many others in the aerospace field, often go on to pursue a PhD.

FACT SHEET

EARTH'S MOON

DIAMETER: *2,159 miles (3,475 kilometers)*

MASS: *0.012 Earth masses*

AVERAGE DISTANCE FROM THE SUN: *1 AU*

KNOWN MOONS: *0*

LENGTH OF DAY: *29.5 Earth days (708.7 hours)*

LENGTH OF YEAR: *1 Earth year (365.25 days)*

AVERAGE TEMPERATURE: *–4 degrees Fahrenheit (–20 degrees Celsius)*

The Moon is much smaller than Earth, but it is still the largest moon in the solar system relative to its planet. Our moon has essentially no atmosphere. It is the only other body in the solar system that humans have stood upon.

The Earth's Moon

Our Moon's gravity causes most of Earth's tides, though the Sun also contributes. Tides have led the Moon to be in synchronous locked rotation with the Earth. That means the same side of the Moon always faces the Earth.

There have been several theories for the origin of the Moon. The generally accepted theory is that the

Moon formed when something made a giant impact on the Earth long, long ago. We're talking a small planet-size body hitting the Earth and stripping off a good portion of the Earth's less-dense outer layer. Most of the material fell back to Earth, but some of it combined into what we see as the Moon today. Rocks brought back from the Moon have supported this theory.

Astronaut Harrison Schmitt next to a lunar boulder

THE MOON'S SURFACE AND STRUCTURE

When you look at the Moon with just your eyes, you can see dark regions and light regions. Light regions are the highlands, which are older. The dark regions are known as the mare (MAR-ay). This comes from the Latin word for seas because that's what some people thought they were. They're actually large flows of lava that happened around three billion years ago, which is still much later than when the highlands formed. The mare often filled in giant impact craters, which is why many of them look circular.

The Moon's surface is dominated by impact craters. They range in size from microscopic to hundreds of miles and can exist for billions of years. The Moon has given us important insights into the early solar system and the importance of impact.

Heavily cratered surface of the Moon

Each lunar daytime is about fourteen Earth days long and each night is the same. Like Mercury, the Moon reaches very high temperatures from long periods in daylight with no atmosphere and a fluffy surface. At night, for the same reason, the surface cools drastically. Surface temperatures vary by hundreds of degrees from daytime to nighttime. Also like Mercury, there are permanently shadowed craters in the polar regions that contain water ice.

The Moon has a simpler structure than Earth in terms of its interior. Being smaller, it cooled more over the history of the solar system. This resulted in an interior that is largely solid. There is no magnetic field to protect the surface from impacts of the charged particles of the solar wind.

The Moon gets farther from the Earth each year at about the same rate that your fingernails grow, about 1.5 inches (3.8 centimeters) per year. This is because tides take energy out of the system. (Remember that tides are a result of the gravitational tugging between the Earth and the Moon.) Another effect of this is the slowing of Earth's rotation over time. The Earth's day used to be shorter. The changes are tiny and take place over a long time, but a few hundred million years ago, the day was actually 22 hours long rather than 24.

PHASES OF THE MOON

Moon phases showing orbital locations

The Moon goes around the Earth over the course of about a month. During that time, we see it go through different phases. When all the places we can see on the Moon experience daytime, it causes a full moon. When we see portions in day and portions in night, it makes the Moon appear as different shapes.

Full moon occurs when the Moon is on the opposite side of Earth from the Sun. New moon occurs when it is between the Earth and the Sun. First quarter and third quarter moons occur when half of what we see is in daytime and half of it is in nighttime.

MARGARET HAMILTON *(born 1936)* was a pioneer in computer software programming. She worked on the Apollo missions that landed humans on the Moon. In the 1960s, she studied at the Massachusetts Institute of Technology (MIT). There were no classes on computer coding back then, so people learned as they went. During that time, MIT created some of the software for the Apollo program. Hamilton led a team that developed software for the Command Module that took the astronauts into space and back. This team also worked on the Lunar Module that landed on the Moon. This software was designed to navigate the spacecraft and control things like small rocket thrusters to guide its path. Hamilton herself worked on software to detect errors and recover from computer crashes. Her work enabled the successful landing of humans on the Moon and returned them safely to Earth.

KEY FIGURES IN HISTORY

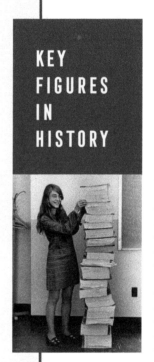

Margaret Hamilton with Apollo software printouts

MARS

DIAMETER: *4,221 miles (6,792 kilometers)*

MASS: *0.11 Earth masses*

AVERAGE DISTANCE FROM THE SUN: *1.52 AU*

KNOWN MOONS: *2*

LENGTH OF DAY: *1.03 Earth days (24.7 hours)*

LENGTH OF YEAR: *1.88 Earth years (687.0 days)*

AVERAGE TEMPERATURE: *-85 degrees Fahrenheit (-65 degrees Celsius)*

Mars with polar cap at top

Mars (MAARZ), known as the Red Planet, is the fourth planet from the Sun. It appears as a reddish-orange, starlike object in the night sky. The distance between Mars and Earth varies considerably because of the movement in their orbits. That's why Mars goes from somewhat bright to extremely bright. The ancient Romans named the planet after their god of war because its reddish color reminded them of blood.

Mars is significantly smaller than Earth but much larger than Mercury. A day on Mars is only about forty minutes longer than Earth's. Because Mars is about

50 percent farther from the Sun than Earth, it receives much less sunlight and has very cold temperatures.

Like Earth, Mars has channels, canyons, volcanoes, and icy polar caps. Despite these scenic features, Mars is still an unpleasant place. Its thin atmosphere almost completely lacks oxygen, and for the past few billion years, it hasn't had a significant amount of liquid water. Nonetheless, Mars is a prime destination for exploration and science because of its amazing geology, complex history, and active atmosphere.

MARS'S ATMOSPHERE

Mars had a much thicker atmosphere in the past, but now it is very thin. This is because its lower gravity does not hold on to the atmosphere as tightly and the planet has been bombarded by solar wind. This is all compounded by a lack of a magnetic field later in Mars's history.

Despite how thin it is, the atmosphere has circulation patterns, wind, and clouds. The clouds are either water ice or carbon dioxide ice, which is what we call dry ice on Earth. Mars also has dust storms.

Clouds over Mars

The surface pressure on Mars is less than 1 percent of the surface pressure on Earth. Its density is similar to the thin air 100,000 feet (30 kilometers) above the surface of the Earth. Its atmosphere is 95 percent carbon dioxide, the gas we exhale and use to make bubbles in carbonated soft drinks.

Carbon dioxide behaves on Mars like it does on the Earth: It goes from a solid to a gas and from a gas to a solid with no liquid phase. Unlike on Earth, water on Mars behaves in this same way due to the low pressures and cold temperatures. There is no sustained liquid water on the surface of Mars.

MARS'S SURFACE

Helicopter on surface of Mars

When the NASA *Viking* **landers** made it to Mars in 1976, the pictures they took showed rocks, sand, and dust. Much of what was seen was red due to oxidized iron minerals—essentially, rust. If all you did was take a quick look at those lander pictures, you might think Mars's surface looks pretty simple. But it's actually geologically complex. The oldest surfaces in the southern highlands date from 3.5 to 4 billion years ago, when there was frequent impact cratering. The younger areas, often in the northern lowlands or on the huge volcanoes, are much younger. They're still very old, though, with most ages ranging from one to three billion years.

Water-cut delta on Mars

Many places on Mars show evidence of liquid water flow in the past, from enormous flood channels to river-like and delta-like structures. They preserve a fascinating era under a thicker atmosphere.

Mars also has polar caps. These icy deposits surround the north and south poles. On Earth, our polar caps are water ice. On Mars, water ice forms the base of the polar caps. Huge dry-ice polar caps grow each winter and dissipate in the summer, except for a smaller dry-ice cap in the south.

FUN FACT

The surface area of Mars is about equal to the land surface area of the Earth—in other words, without the oceans—so exploring the surface of Mars is equivalent to exploring the entire land surface of the Earth. This is why we use orbiters to study large areas of the planet. We can put only a limited number of landers and rovers on the surface because they're expensive and complicated. Even the rovers explore only a few miles at most during their lifetime. This is also why scientists spend a lot of effort carefully choosing the best landing sites.

The Curiosity rover taking a selfie on Mars

MARS'S STRUCTURE

Mars's interior structure

Like the other terrestrial planets, Mars's internal structure has a core at the center, a mantle, and an outer crust. Because Mars is smaller than Earth, the interior has cooled more over time. This has created more solid material and less liquid material. It's probably also the reason why Mars has no internally driven magnetic field. But there is evidence that points to Mars having had one in the past.

The farther you get away from a magnetic field, the harder it becomes to detect and the less effect it has over anything. You've probably noticed this with refrigerator magnets—they don't start pulling toward the refrigerator until you get close enough. When NASA flew the *Mars Global Surveyor* in 1997, its orbit was lower than previous orbits, and its magnetic field sensors were more sensitive than prior ones. This allowed us for the first time to detect magnetic fields on the planet. They were frozen into the surface rocks in some locations. When those surface rocks came out as lava, the iron inside oriented with the magnetic field of the planet. The rock still preserves the magnetic field as a result. All this indicates that Mars probably had an internally driven magnetic field in the distant past.

NOTEWORTHY FEATURES

The largest mountain in the solar system is a volcano on Mars: Olympus Mons (uh-LIM-puhs MAANS). The volcano is about 2.5 times higher than Mount Everest and is as wide as the state of Arizona. It is made

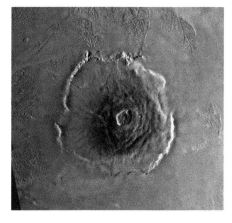

Olympus Mons

of basalt lava, similar to the Hawaiian islands. Another way in which Olympus Mons is similar to the Hawaiian islands is its so-called shield volcano shape. It has very low slopes and runny lava that spreads out over a *huge* area.

The largest canyon system in the solar system is on Mars, too. This system is called Valles Marineris (VAL-uhs mar-uh-NAIR-is). It is named after the *Mariner 9* spacecraft, which was the first to study Mars. If Valles Marineris were on Earth, it would stretch all the way across the United States from the Pacific Ocean to the Atlantic Ocean. The Grand Canyon would appear as a small crack in one little piece on the edge. The formation of Valles Marineris was very complex over a long period of time. It involved water erosion, the canyon pulling apart, the filling of the canyon with deposits, and the erosion of those deposits. In other words, general chaos over billions of years.

Valles Marineris (United States for scale)

Are we alone in the universe? Mysteries don't get much bigger than that. Science fiction often focuses on intelligent life and whether it exists elsewhere in the universe. But there's also the question of simple **microbial life**, such as bacteria and viruses. Did it or any other form of life start elsewhere in our own solar system? Mars has been one of the places scientists are most interested in studying to find answers to this question.

Water provides and sustains life on Earth. The past presence of liquid water on Mars, and lots of it, makes scientists wonder if there could've been past life on Mars. There is no strong evidence for this at the moment. And, to be clear, it would probably be microbial life and nothing as advanced as humanoid Martians. Orbiters and rovers have established that Mars had habitable environments in the past. The *Perseverance* rover landed in 2021 to search for any evidence that might indicate past life.

MARS'S MOONS

Mars has two small moons, Phobos (FOH-bohs) and Deimos (DEE-mohs). Each is irregularly shaped and about the size of a large city. The length of Phobos is about 16 miles (26 kilometers), and the length of Deimos is 9 miles (16 kilometers). They basically look like potatoes. They are rocky objects with old surfaces covered in craters. They may be asteroids that were captured into the orbit of Mars.

The moons were discovered in 1877 by American astronomer Asaph Hall. He had been actively searching for Martian moons using a telescope at the U.S. Naval Observatory in Washington, DC. They were hard to observe because they're small and remain relatively close to Mars. The moons are named after ancient Greek gods. Phobos is the god of fear and panic, and Deimos is the god of dread and terror. In ancient Greek mythology, Phobos and Deimos were the sons of Ares, the god of war. Ares is the Greek equivalent of the Roman god Mars.

Phobos orbits very low to the planet at an altitude of around 3,721 miles (6,000 kilometers). It takes only eight hours for Phobos to orbit Mars. Deimos orbits

Phobos

higher up in a thirty-hour orbit. By comparison, our Moon takes about twenty-seven days to orbit Earth. Although Phobos goes in the same direction as Mars's rotation, it rises in the west and sets in the east. This is because Phobos orbits faster than Mars rotates. The moon passes overhead in just a few minutes. Phobos is gradually getting closer to Mars. It is predicted to either crash into Mars in 50 million years or break apart.

Stickney is the largest crater on Phobos. It is named for Asaph Hall's wife's maiden name. The crater is so large it likely almost broke Phobos apart. At 5.6 miles (9 kilometers) in diameter, Stickney is about half the diameter of the entire moon of Phobos. The largest crater on Deimos is only 1.4 miles (2.3 kilometers) in diameter. That's about one-fourth the size of the Stickney crater.

Both Phobos and Deimos have fluffy surfaces that have been beaten up by impact over billions of years. The surfaces heat and cool very quickly on both moons. Temperatures range from 25 degrees Fahrenheit (−4 degrees Celsius) to −170 degrees Fahrenheit (−112 degrees Celsius).

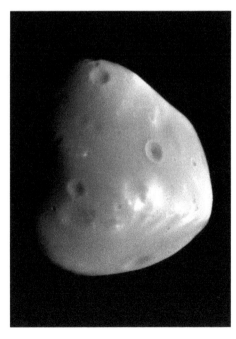

Deimos

FUN FACT

Mars has partial solar eclipses. From parts of the planet during some seasons, both Phobos and Deimos pass in front of the Sun as seen from the surface of Mars. Phobos covers about two-thirds of the Sun during the largest portion of the eclipse. The eclipse itself lasts less than 20 seconds because of how fast Phobos moves in the sky. Deimos covers less of the Sun but is still noticeable. Orbiters can see the shadows from these eclipses on the surface of Mars. Cameras on the *Opportunity* rover in the 2000s and the *Curiosity* rover in the 2010s have been used to capture images of these eclipses.

Phobos passing in front of the Sun

ASTEROIDS

Put simply, asteroids are rocks in space. They can range from tens of feet in diameter to hundreds of miles.

Most asteroids exist in the asteroid belt, a very wide and large doughnut-shaped area between the orbit of Mars and the orbit of Jupiter. There are hundreds of millions of objects in the asteroid belt,

Vesta, one of the largest asteroids

but if you squished all of them together into a ball, that ball would still be smaller than the Earth's Moon. The mass of all the objects in the asteroid belt is less than 4 percent of the mass of the Moon.

Some of the largest asteroids are Vesta, Pallas, and Hygeia, each a few hundred miles in diameter. The largest object in the asteroid belt is the dwarf planet Ceres.

Science fiction movies often depict asteroid belts as a tight collection of rocks in space. In reality, most of the asteroid belt is quite empty, and the average distance between the asteroids is large.

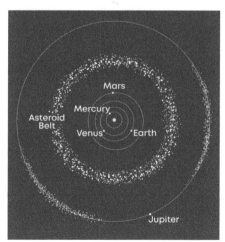

Orbits of inner planets, Jupiter, and the asteroid belt

TYPES OF ASTEROIDS

Asteroids come in a wide variety of types. They are categorized by their surface composition. There are three main categories. The first type is carbon-rich asteroids, also known as carbonaceous or C-type. Second are silica-rich or S-type asteroids. The third category is metallic or M-type. The first two categories are primarily rocky. M-type are, as the name suggests, made of significant percentages of metal.

The asteroid Gaspra

Asteroids also come in a variety of physical structures, ranging from solid rock or metal to loosely held-together collections of boulders. Some are even like fluff balls.

Another way we classify asteroids is by the position of their orbits in the solar system. Asteroid-belt asteroids are also called main-belt asteroids. There are asteroids that orbit close to our planet, which are called near-Earth asteroids. Trojan asteroids share an orbit with the planet Jupiter. Centaurs are asteroids that orbit between Jupiter and Neptune.

It is thought that about 66 million years ago, an asteroid or comet 6 to 9 miles (10 to 15 kilometers) in diameter slammed into Earth and caused the extinction of the dinosaurs and 70 percent of all species on Earth. Fortunately, an object that big strikes Earth on average only every few hundred million years based on evidence in our geological records.

In 1908, an asteroid entered the atmosphere and exploded above a remote region in Siberia, Russia. The shock wave destroyed around 770 square miles (2,000 square kilometers) of forest. That's about 1.5 times the size of the city of Los Angeles. This impact is known as the Tunguska event, named after a nearby river. Luckily the region was so remote that, to our knowledge, no humans were hurt. You needn't worry though: Tunguska-size impacts only occur once every many hundreds of years on average. Space agencies and astronomers continue to work on preventing them.

ASTEROID ORIGINS

Accretion occurred in the region where the asteroid belt now exists. Particles of dust would hit and stick together and form bigger particles that stick together. In other parts of the solar system, this process of accretion eventually formed planets. But not in the region that would become the asteroid belt. The effects of Jupiter's enormous gravity increased the velocities of the objects that were forming. This caused collisions that broke things apart rather than sticking them together.

When asteroids were first discovered in the 1800s, there was a theory that the asteroid belt was one planet that had shattered. The reality is more complex. The low mass of everything in the asteroid belt combined with the variable compositions argues against that shattered-planet theory. Asteroids in the asteroid

Main-belt asteroid Ida and its moon, Dactyl

belt are really leftovers of the original formation of the solar system. They're basically things that didn't become something bigger and didn't get ejected by gravity outward in the solar system.

METEOROIDS, METEORS, AND METEORITES

Asteroids sometimes smash into each other during their orbit. When this happens, smaller pieces of asteroid can break off into space. Meteoroids are objects in space smaller than an asteroid, which means smaller than several feet in diameter.

Near-Earth asteroid Bennu

If a meteoroid comes close enough to Earth, it heats up and glows from hitting the Earth's atmosphere. The streak of light that results is called a meteor. You might have heard them referred to as shooting stars, even though they aren't stars.

Some meteoroids make it all the way through the atmosphere and land on Earth. Any rock that makes it to the surface of the Earth is called a meteorite. Most meteorites are fragments of asteroids. There are 190 known impact craters on our planet, but dangerous impacts happen very rarely.

SPACE IN DAILY LIFE

One way we use space technology in our daily lives is through mapping. Software on computers, phones, and other devices can tell you almost exactly where you are and how to get where you want to go. This is all thanks to Global Positioning System (GPS) satellites. There are more than thirty satellites in orbit that transmit signals to provide us with this information. Originally designed and flown by the U.S. military in the 1970s, GPS was opened to civilian use and started becoming common in the 1990s. Your computer or phone receives input from multiple GPS satellites at the same time. Then software uses the satellite positions and geometry to calculate where you are. This is all enabled by the work and research developed for spaceflight. These technological advancements didn't only fly spacecraft but also enabled us to know precise positions and orbits.

CERES

Ceres (SAIR-ees) is the largest object in the asteroid belt and the first to be discovered in 1801. After it was found by Italian astronomer Giuseppe Piazzi, it was classified as a planet. But many other objects were discovered in the same region, what we now know as the asteroid belt. British-German astronomer William Herschel believed they belonged to a new category of space object. In 1802, he invented the word *asteroid*, which is what we eventually called Ceres. But that wasn't the last time Ceres would be reclassified.

With the creation of the term *dwarf planet* in 2006, Ceres became the only dwarf planet that spends all its time inside the orbit of Neptune. Technically, it still can be called the largest asteroid. Although it has been called different things, the name *Ceres* has remained. It is named for the Roman goddess of grains and harvests.

Ceres from the Dawn *spacecraft*

Ceres has been a popular location for science fiction books, movies, TV shows, and video games. It was featured in numerous novels of the twentieth century and continues to show up in popular culture today. More recently it was a major space station and base for humans in "The Expanse" series of books as well as a television show based on the books. It appears in the video game *Destiny*, where it was inhabited by creatures called the Fallen and eventually destroyed by a species called the Awoken.

CERES IS NO ASTEROID

Ceres orbits about 2.8 AU from the Sun. By far the largest object in the asteroid belt, it has about 25 percent of the entire region's mass. At a diameter of about 600 miles (1,000 kilometers), it's the only object in the asteroid belt that is massive enough to have formed into a rounded, nearly spherical body. Its surface temperatures range from about −260 to −40 degrees Fahrenheit (−160 to −40 degrees Celsius).

Ceres is heavily cratered, indicating an old age for most of its surface. But it has interesting younger features that were only discovered when the *Dawn* spacecraft went into orbit around Ceres starting in 2015. *Dawn* was the first spacecraft to visit a dwarf planet.

Images of Ceres show a small number of bright white spots on its dark gray surface. These mysterious spots, called faculae, are now thought to be salts. They're not your typical table salt, which is sodium chloride. The faculae are mostly sodium carbonate and ammonium chloride. The spots likely formed from salty waters coming out from under the surface. When they reached the surface, the water turned to gas and left behind all the salt.

Occator crater on Ceres

The largest mountain on Ceres is Ahuna Mons. It is 16,000 feet (4,876 meters) high and thought to have formed by a process called cryovolcanism. This is when materials erupt into an environment with extremely cold temperatures. During the process, salty, muddy water ice moved upward and created a mountain.

Jupiter, Saturn, Uranus, and Neptune

GAS GIANTS AND ICE GIANTS

The outer solar system has four planets: Jupiter, Saturn, Uranus, and Neptune. Being farther from the Sun, they have much longer orbits. They are known as giant planets because, well, they're huge! Even the smallest, Neptune, could fit more than fifty-seven Earths inside it. They each have many moons and a **ring system**.

These planets do not have a solid surface. Jupiter and Saturn are made of gas, so they're known as gas giants. Uranus and Neptune are ice giants, mostly made of materials that would have been ice when the planet was forming. The ice giants are much smaller than the gas giants.

JUPITER

DIAMETER: *88,846 miles (142,984 kilometers)*

MASS: *317.83 Earth masses*

AVERAGE DISTANCE FROM THE SUN: *5.2 AU*

KNOWN MOONS: *80*

LENGTH OF DAY: *0.414 Earth days (9.93 hours)*

LENGTH OF YEAR: *11.86 Earth years (4,333 days)*

AVERAGE TEMPERATURE: *–162 degrees Fahrenheit (–108 degrees Celsius)*

Jupiter's clouds and Great Red Spot

Jupiter (JOO-pih-tr) is the fifth planet from the Sun and by far the largest. More than 1,000 Earths could fit inside Jupiter. It has 2.5 times more mass than all the other planets combined. It is named after the ruler of the Roman gods. Known as a gas giant planet, it is composed almost entirely of hydrogen with some helium.

Jupiter is the third brightest natural object in the night sky after the Moon and Venus. It has white and reddish stripes as well as its famous storm system, the Great Red Spot. It has an elaborate system of moons as well as faint rings.

Jupiter is about five times farther from the Sun than the Earth. It takes about twelve Earth years to go around the Sun. Jupiter rotates the fastest of any planet in the solar system, with one day lasting about ten hours.

JUPITER'S ATMOSPHERE

Jupiter's atmosphere is almost entirely hydrogen gas, which is the lightest gas and what makes up most of the Sun. There is also a significant amount of helium. Smaller amounts of other molecules such as water and ammonia are also present.

The atmosphere has alternating dark belts and bright zones with winds moving in opposite directions and areas of turbulence in between. There are also many huge storm systems on Jupiter, the most well known being the Great Red Spot. This storm system is like a hurricane or cyclone on Earth but much larger—our entire planet could fit inside it. It has been around and observed by telescopes for more than 300 years. Like storms on Earth, it changes details of its shape and rotates. Over the past 150 years, it has been shrinking in size while simultaneously growing taller. It extends hundreds of miles deep into the atmosphere.

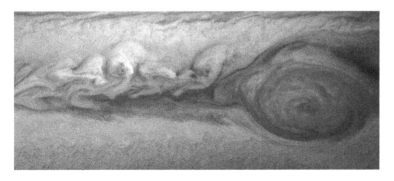

The Great Red Spot

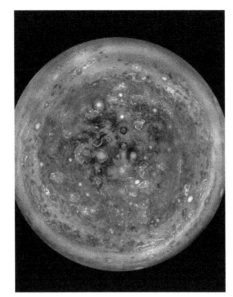

There are numerous other oval and circular storms. Some are white, and some are reddish brown. They last much longer than Earth storms because there is no surface to interact with and remove energy. Lightning has also been observed on Jupiter.

FUN FACT

Jupiter's powerful gravity has been used by numerous spacecraft to change their speeds and directions. This technique is called a gravity assist. The spacecraft gets targeted so that the gravity of a planet or other body combines with that body's velocity to change the spacecraft's orbit. Gravity assists were used by *Pioneer*, *Voyager*, and *Cassini* spacecraft to head to Saturn. The *Ulysses* spacecraft headed out to Jupiter, but not to visit the planet. Instead, it used the gravity to orbit over the poles of the Sun. It headed all the way out in order to head in!

JUPITER'S STRUCTURE

There is no solid surface on Jupiter. The upper atmosphere is mostly hydrogen, which is in a gas state. As pressures get higher inside Jupiter, the hydrogen turns to a liquid. And even deeper in the high-pressure interior, hydrogen becomes a very unusual material called metallic hydrogen. That's when hydrogen acts like a metal with its electrons running around so it can conduct electricity. There may be a rocky core at the very center that is the size of one to two Earths.

The faster rotation of Jupiter combined with all that metallic hydrogen generates the solar system's largest planetary magnetic field. The magnetosphere, the sphere of influence of Jupiter's magnetic field, extends millions of miles toward the

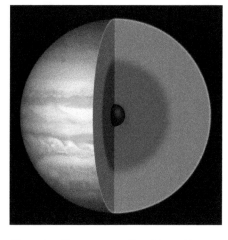

Interior of Jupiter

■ *Core (rock, ice)*

■ *Metallic hydrogen*

■ *Molecular hydrogen*

Sun. It extends even further in the opposite direction from the Sun, reaching hundreds of millions of miles after being pushed out by solar wind. The so-called tail of the magnetosphere is so huge that it crosses Saturn's orbit. Closer to the planet, including the region of the inner moons, charged particles trapped in the magnetic field can damage spacecraft electronics. Spacecraft either limit their time in this region or have electronics that are specially designed and shielded to survive.

JUPITER'S RINGS

Jupiter has rings like the rest of the giant planets. But unlike the spectacular rings of Saturn, Jupiter has only a few rings. They are very faint and mostly made of dust. Jupiter's rings likely came from impacts into the planet's small innermost moons. Those impacts would have kicked out dust into Jupiter's orbit.

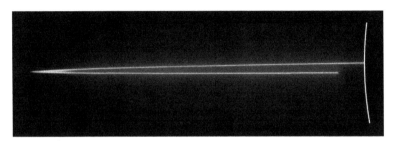

Jupiter's backlit main ring and upper atmosphere

In 1993, fragments of a comet were discovered orbiting Jupiter. Previously, the comet had passed close enough to Jupiter for the planet's gravity to rip it apart into twenty-one distinct pieces. This comet, or its fragments, was called Shoemaker-Levy 9. It was named after the scientists who discovered it, Gene and Carolyn Shoemaker and David Levy. It was the ninth comet they discovered, hence the number 9.

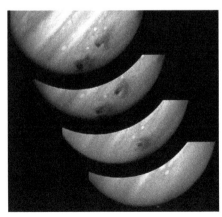

Evolution of impact "scars" from Shoemaker-Levy 9 comet

In 1994, the astronomy world became very excited when calculations showed the twenty-one pieces would slam into Jupiter at high speeds. Observatories around the world, as well as spacecraft in favorable positions, were all observing Jupiter when it happened. Many predicted there would be little to see. However, we saw an incredible demonstration of the power of impact. Material was dredged up from within the atmosphere, and what looked like bruises were visible on Jupiter even through small telescopes. Some were as large as the diameter of three Earths. They stayed visible for months.

CAREERS IN ASTRONOMY

Not only scientists and engineers work in the field of space science. There are many different careers in communication and public outreach. These jobs are responsible for communicating science to the public. There are journalists who write for newspapers, magazines, or the web; authors who write books; and people who create videos for social media. Outside of publishing and media, there are also communications careers. They include duties like writing press releases about scientific results. Planetariums around the world also share the joys of space with the public, and there are various careers in those facilities. Then, of course, there are teachers at all levels of schooling who teach about astronomy and space science.

Many of these people have college science degrees. But some may have studied journalism, communications, or English literature. Some may be scientists or engineers who dedicate some or all of their time to communicating with the public.

JUPITER'S MOONS

As of 2021, Jupiter is known to have eighty moons. More continue to be discovered. Jupiter's moons are typically named after mythological lovers or daughters of the Roman god Jupiter or his Greek equivalent, Zeus.

There are four small moons that orbit between Jupiter and the Galilean moons, the four largest moons. All eight of these inner moons have nearly circular orbits in Jupiter's **equatorial plane**, like a miniature solar system. The other seventy-two moons are very small. They have a wide range of more distant orbits. These so-called irregular moons are likely asteroids captured by Jupiter's gravity.

The Galilean moons are some of the largest bodies in the solar system. They are all larger than Pluto, the largest dwarf planet. Ganymede is the largest moon in the solar system and is larger than Mercury. The Galilean moons are so big that they would be considered planets or dwarf planets if they did not orbit Jupiter. They contain 99.997 percent of the mass of the Jupiter moon system—almost the entire system. In other words, they are *much* bigger than the other moons.

Io, Europa, Ganymede, and Callisto

The Galilean moons, or Galilean satellites, were the first objects observed to not orbit the Earth or the Sun. All are named after lovers of Zeus, the Greek equivalent of Jupiter. They are easily visible as tiny dots of light next to Jupiter when viewed through a small telescope or even steadily held binoculars. You can observe them moving from night to night.

IO

Io (EYE-oh or EE-oh) is the innermost Galilean moon, orbiting Jupiter in about 1.8 days. As such, it gets pulled by Jupiter's gravity and by the other Galilean moons so that it flexes like a ball being squeezed. That causes the interior

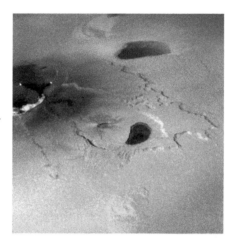

Volcanic eruption on Io

to heat up, which creates the most volcanically active body in the solar system. There are hundreds of active volcanoes on Io.

Io's surface comes in a wide range of colors, from white to yellow to orange to black. The dark colors are caused by silicate rock, the kind we are used to on Earth. It also has sulfur-based volcanic activity, which causes many of the exotic colors. Plumes of sulfur dioxide ice extend hundreds of miles above the surface and then fall back as sulfur dioxide snow. Io has a very thin atmosphere because of the effects from all the volcanoes.

EUROPA

Europa (yer-OPE-uh) is the next Galilean moon out from Jupiter. It orbits in about 3.5 Earth days. Europa is somewhat smaller than Io and covered in water ice, lots of cracks, and a range of other features.

Europa is particularly intriguing because it probably has a liquid-water ocean. The ocean lies underneath several miles of ice. It is thought to have twice the volume of all of Earth's oceans combined. We think there's a rocky ocean floor, which may have some underwater volcanic activity and vents that circulate hot water. These same conditions facilitate life at vents on the ocean floor of the Earth, which makes us wonder if there could be life in the Europa ocean.

Recent observations have shown there is possible water vapor coming out of Europa. This may indicate material coming out from the ocean from an eruption. As of 2021, Europa will be a focus of at least two spacecraft missions in the 2020s and 2030s.

Possible interior structure of Europa

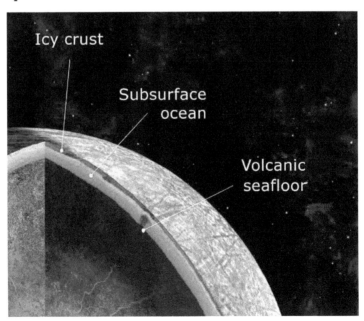

Icy crust

Subsurface ocean

Volcanic seafloor

GANYMEDE

Ganymede (GA-nuh-meed) takes seven days to orbit. This moon has two very different terrains on its surface: an older, rockier dark terrain and a brighter, icier terrain. It may also have an ocean below its surface. It is thought that this salty ocean helps it generate its own magnetic field separate from Jupiter's.

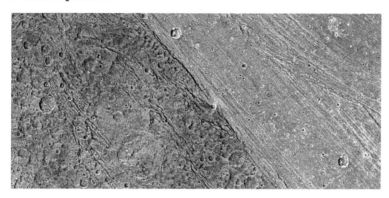

Terrains of Ganymede

CALLISTO

Callisto (kuh-LIH-stow) orbits in seventeen days and has one of the most heavily cratered surfaces in the solar system. This suggests that its surface is mostly very old. This moon is dark in appearance, similar to Ganymede's darker terrain. There are rocky and icy materials on Callisto's terrain, and it may have a liquid-water ocean underneath the surface.

Callisto from Voyager 1

SATURN

DIAMETER: *74,897 miles (120,536 kilometers)*

MASS: *95 Earth masses*

AVERAGE DISTANCE FROM THE SUN: *9.6 AU*

KNOWN MOONS: *83*

LENGTH OF DAY: *0.45 Earth day (10.7 hours)*

LENGTH OF YEAR: *29.4 Earth years (10,747 days)*

AVERAGE TEMPERATURE: *–220 degrees Fahrenheit (–140 degrees Celsius)*

Saturn (SA-tern) is the sixth planet from the Sun and the second largest in the solar system. It is a gas giant, made mostly of hydrogen. Saturn appears yellowish with stripes of slightly varying colors parallel to the equator. But the most interesting thing about its appearance is its elaborate rings.

Saturn is easily visible in the night sky, appearing as a fairly bright star that looks slightly yellow. You can see its rings if you use even a small telescope.

Saturn and its rings

The orbit of Saturn is nearly thirty years because it's about twelve times farther from the Sun than Earth. Saturn has the second shortest day in the solar system, only 10.7 hours long. Its axis is tilted at a similar angle to Earth, which means it has seasons like our planet. Saturn is named after the Roman god of wealth and agriculture, who was also the father of Jupiter.

SATURN'S ATMOSPHERE

Saturn's atmosphere consists of stripes called belts and zones, like Jupiter's but wider. They have subtle differences in color but are mostly yellowish due to ammonia ice clouds. The second highest wind speeds in the solar system

White clouds from a gigantic storm on Saturn

are on Saturn. They reach up to 1,100 miles per hour (1,770 kilometers per hour) in the equatorial region. That's about five times faster than the highest hurricane winds on Earth!

Large-scale storms happen periodically on Saturn. Occasionally they hit the upper atmosphere where we are able to see them. In 2011, one of these storms appeared as turbulent white clouds that eventually stretched around the planet. The storm was clearly visible in telescopes for many months.

Saturn's north polar region has a hexagon-shaped jet stream cloud feature. First discovered by the

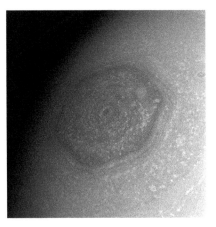

Saturn's north polar hexagon

Voyager spacecraft in the 1980s, it still exists to this day. The jet stream has 200-mile-per-hour (320-kilometer-per-hour) winds that make their way around the pole. It is also enormous, about 20,000 miles (32,000 kilometers) across. At the center of Saturn's polar hexagon is an enormous storm called the north polar vortex. The eye of this storm is about 1,200 miles (2,000 kilometers) across.

FUN FACT

When the *Cassini* spacecraft flew by Saturn in 2013, it captured over 300 images during a four-hour period. At this time, *Cassini* was positioned behind Saturn relative to the Sun. Of these images, 141 were put together to produce a huge mosaic called *The Day the Earth Smiled*. The picture shows a stunning backlit Saturn and the ring system. You can see the Earth, the Moon, Venus, and Mars in the picture, too—they appear as tiny dots. When the spacecraft was taking pictures, NASA encouraged people on Earth to look up and smile for the camera. This was a symbolic gesture, because the Earth wasn't more than a blue pixel.

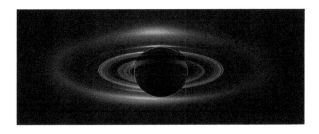

Saturn backlit by the Sun

SATURN'S STRUCTURE

The two gas giants in our solar system have similar structures. Saturn's is smaller than Jupiter's, but that doesn't mean it's a small planet. You could fit over 760 Earths inside Saturn—and that's not even counting the rings.

The outer layer of Saturn is its atmosphere, which is almost entirely hydrogen. There is also a small percentage of helium, along with ammonia. Lower down there is water that forms ice clouds.

When the pressures from above become high enough, the hydrogen and helium become liquids. This creates the next layer down. Below that, Saturn has enough pressure to create metallic hydrogen. This is the same material

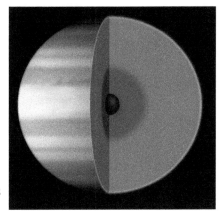

Interior of Saturn

■ *Core (rock, ice)*

■ *Metallic hydrogen*

■ *Molecular hydrogen*

inside Jupiter. And like Jupiter, the metallic hydrogen inside Saturn combines with the rotation of the planet to create a large magnetic field. Beneath that is a core that is likely a mixture of iron, nickel, and rock. Although this core is small compared to Saturn's, it is still bigger than the entire Earth.

Though its interior is high density, the overall average density of Saturn is the lowest of any planet in the solar system. It is a little less dense than water, so if you had a big enough swimming pool, Saturn would be able to float in it.

SATURN'S RINGS

Saturn is famous for its beautiful ring system. Much brighter and more extensive than any of the other planet's ring systems, it consists of billions of dirty snowballs made from water ice. The particles making up the rings range in size. They can be as small as dust or as big as a house. Some are even as large as mountains!

Some of the first telescopes observed Saturn in the 1600s. These observations led some to believe there were solid handles on the side of Saturn. When telescopes were improved, the "handles" were seen as four large rings. But it turns out those rings are made up of hundreds of rings. And there are additional fainter rings among the main rings. If you drove at the edge of Saturn's rings system at 60 miles per hour

Saturn's rings seen from Cassini

(100 kilometers per hour), it would take about a year to make it all the way around.

The rings are in line with Saturn's equator, orbiting between the planet and all its major moons. They are thought to have formed from comets or moons that got close enough to Saturn that its gravity ripped them into smaller pieces.

Saturn's rings are extremely thin compared to their diameter. The main rings are about 30 feet (10 meters) thick and over 40,000 miles (64,000 kilometers) wide.

THE SOLAR SYSTEM'S
BIG MYSTERIES

How old are Saturn's rings? There are wildly different estimates, ranging from 4.5 billion years to only 100 million years. There are two basic theories of their formation, but there are numerous sub-theories. They could have formed along with Saturn like a miniature solar system. Or a moon could have wandered too close to Saturn. The different gravity across the moon would rip it apart and put pieces of material into orbit.

The *Cassini* spacecraft made various observations in the 2000s and 2010s that did not solve the issue but led to many more detailed studies. We know the inner rings are slowly losing material. Some studies work backward from the current estimates of ring loss to determine how long the rings would've been around. Estimates range from many hundreds of millions of years to 100 million years.

SATURN'S MOONS

As of 2021, Saturn was known to have eighty-three moons, though more are being discovered. Titan is by far the largest. But there are six others large enough for their own gravity to shape them into near-spherical bodies. The others are smaller and irregularly shaped. With cold temperatures due to Saturn's distance from the Sun, the moons are dominated by water ice with rocky material.

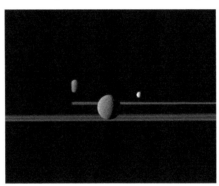

Moons from left: Dione, Rhea, Enceladus

The larger moons all orbit in the equatorial plane of Saturn, which is also the plane of the rings. The moons and rings are effectively a mini solar system. Several of the moons interact with the rings, and some small moons are even within the rings.

Saturn's moons were originally named for Greco-Roman gods. But as scientists discovered more and more, they began using names from Gallic, Inuit, Norse, and other myths.

TITAN

Titan (TAI-tun) is the second-largest moon in the solar system behind Jupiter's Ganymede. It is larger than the entire planet Mercury. Titan is the only moon in the solar system with a thick nitrogen atmosphere. The surface pressure is about 1.5 times the surface pressure on Earth. Titan is the only place in the solar system besides Earth that has stable liquid at the surface. (Spoiler alert: It's not water!)

When the *Voyager* spacecraft flew by Titan in the early 1980s, all its cameras could see was an orange ball of haze. Titan's atmosphere contains a hydrocarbon haze that encircles the moon. It is similar to smog. When the *Cassini*

Titan in near-infrared light

orbiter visited Saturn in 2004, it went equipped with radar and infrared cameras that could see through the clouds. The *Huygens* spacecraft traveled with *Cassini* and was released into Titan's atmosphere. It parachuted down and gave us our first views beneath the haze. The spacecraft even got a picture from the surface.

What we discovered was an amazingly complex geology. This included liquid-cut valleys and even lakes and seas in its polar regions. They are not filled with liquid water, for the extremely cold temperatures on Titan would cause any water on the surface to be ice. That ice

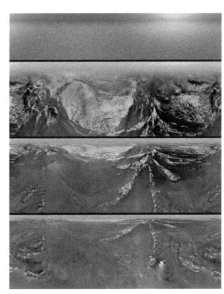

Four images of Titan's surface taken by the Huygens probe at different altitudes

would be more like rock. Instead of water, lakes and seas on Titan are made of liquid hydrocarbons, mostly methane with some ethane. On Earth, we know this combination as natural gas. With the pressures and temperatures of Titan, natural gas can be stable in a liquid phase.

Some of the seas are as large as the Great Lakes on Earth, stretching hundreds of miles wide and hundreds of feet deep. There is a whole equivalent to our water cycle on Earth in these regions. It cycles through natural gas clouds, rain, and lakes.

Titan has a liquid-water ocean below its surface, under miles of ice. It is probably in contact with an ice layer below. The deep interior of Titan is rocky.

FUN FACT

The first *Star Wars* movie released in 1977 introduced us to the Death Star, a space station that was as big as a moon. Three years later, the *Voyager* spacecraft gave us views of a moon of Saturn that looks a lot like the Death Star. This moon is named Mimas (MAI-muss). It has an 80-mile-wide (130-kilometer-wide) crater that is almost one-third the diameter of Mimas. This crater resembles the round weapon on the Death Star's exterior. Mimas has a heavily cratered old surface.

ENCELADUS

Enceladus (en-SEH-leh-duhs) seemed like just
another of Saturn's icy moons. Then the *Cassini*
spacecraft discovered the unexpected: Enceladus
is spewing plumes of water ice and bits of rock
into space! This happens in the moon's south polar
region. From this observation, scientists determined
that Enceladus has a liquid-water ocean under its
icy shell—at least in its south polar region, where the
material was spewing out.

These conditions are similar to what we see on
Earth, where vents in the ocean floor circulate hot
water. We know that this can support life in depths of
the ocean where there is no sunlight. You could say
that Enceladus has the ingredients needed to make

life. That doesn't mean there is life on Enceladus, but it is still an amazing discovery. The energy to drive the activity within Enceladus comes from the tides. On Earth, the tides are influenced by gravity from the Moon and Sun. The force of the tides on Enceladus are caused by Saturn and the moon Dione.

The snowy fallout from Enceladus's water-ice plumes causes it to be the most reflective planetary object in the solar system. Some of the icy particles that do not fall back to the surface end up in orbit around Saturn. They make up one of Saturn's rings.

Water geysers erupting on Enceladus

URANUS

DIAMETER: *31,763 miles (51,118 kilometers)*

MASS: *14.5 Earth masses*

AVERAGE DISTANCE FROM THE SUN: *19.2 AU*

CLOSEST DISTANCE TO EARTH: *17.6 AU*

KNOWN MOONS: *27*

LENGTH OF DAY: *0.72 Earth day (17.2 hours)*

LENGTH OF YEAR: *83.7 Earth years (30,589 days)*

AVERAGE TEMPERATURE: *-320 degrees Fahrenheit (-195 degrees Celsius)*

Uranus (UR-uh-nuss) is one of the giant planets and the seventh planet from the Sun. It is much smaller than Saturn and just slightly larger than Neptune. If Earth were the size of a tennis ball, Uranus would be about the size of a basketball. The planet is named after the Greek god of the sky.

Uranus, as seen by Voyager 2

Along with Neptune, Uranus is known as an ice giant. This is because these planets are mostly made of materials that form ices, such as water, ammonia, and methane.

Uranus was the first planet discovered by telescope in 1781. From a dark site, it is visible with just your eyes. But it was never bright enough to be recognized prior to its telescopic discovery by the astronomer William Herschel.

Compared to other planets, Uranus is tilted sideways. It's the only planet in the solar system that spins on its side relative to its orbit.

URANUS'S ATMOSPHERE

Voyager 2 is the only spacecraft to ever explore Uranus and Neptune. When *Voyager 2* flew by in 1986, Uranus was surprisingly boring. In contrast to other planets with visibly distinguishing features, images showed a plain blue sphere with almost no variation in appearance. But after the launch of the Hubble Space Telescope, the development of more advanced ground telescopes, and the use of other wavelengths to capture images, we were able to observe Uranus over time. Then we found it to have all sorts of things going on.

Uranus with rings and moons

The composition of Uranus's atmosphere is similar to Jupiter and Saturn—mostly hydrogen with some helium. But Uranus, along with Neptune, has more methane. This causes its blue-green color.

The atmosphere of Uranus is heavily affected by seasons. The Uranus year is eighty-four Earth years long, so each season is twenty-one years. Because Uranus rotates on its side compared to its orbit, the poles are pointed toward the Sun and away from the Sun for about twenty-one years.

Voyager 2 arrived at Uranus when its south pole was pointed almost directly at the Sun, so a lot of the planet didn't receive sunlight. Years later in 2007, when both hemispheres were exposed to the Sun, more activity was observed in the atmosphere, such as bright and dark clouds.

FUN FACT

Because of the way its name is spelled and sometimes pronounced, Uranus has been, well, the butt of many jokes. Keeping to this theme, here are two related facts:

It would take about 50 billion rolls of toilet paper to reach Uranus from Earth—that's using standard-size two-ply rolls.

Let's take the scale of the solar system into consideration. If the Sun were at the top of your head and Pluto at the bottom of your feet, Uranus would be right where you'd expect it to be.

URANUS'S STRUCTURE

Uranus and Neptune used to be called gas giants. That was until we realized that they are different from their larger gas-dominated cousins, Jupiter and Saturn. By mass, Uranus is mostly made of so-called ices, including water, methane, and ammonia. In contrast, the gas giants are mostly hydrogen with some helium. The word *ice* in ice giants is a little misleading. The materials that came together to form the ice giants were likely ice when they were forming, but they now exist mostly in a fluid form.

The atmosphere of Uranus is composed of hydrogen, helium, and methane as well as small amounts of other materials. Below that, there is a large region of water with ammonia and methane that exists in a high-pressure fluid form. Deeper down, there is a rocky core.

Interior of Uranus

■ *Core (rock, ice)*

▨ *Mantle (water, ammonia, methane ices)*

▨ *Hydrogen, helium, methane gas*

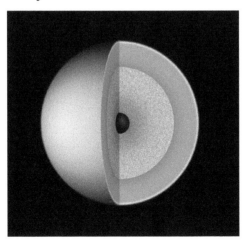

Like the other giant planets, Uranus has a significant magnetic field that is generated from its interior. But unlike these planets, the magnetic fielded of Uranus is crooked. It is tilted about 60 degrees from the spin axis. It's also off-center by about one-third of a radius.

URANUS'S RINGS

Uranus is known to have thirteen rings. The inner eleven rings are very narrow and extremely dark. They are thought to be mostly water ice, but with dark material on the surface. That darkness is likely due to what is essentially dirt with carbon in it. The dark material is likely darkened even more by charged particles moving through the planet's magnetosphere. This causes a darkening effect when the particles interact with the dirt.

The rings of Uranus are thought to be several hundred million years old. That means they're significantly younger than the solar system. They may have resulted from the breakup of moons due to impact. When this happened, the broken-up material may have spread out and formed the rings. Uranus's rings are not like Jupiter's dusty ring nor like Saturn's mostly bright, icy rings.

The outer two rings were discovered only in the early 2000s using observations from the Hubble Space Telescope. The innermost of these two rings is reddish like dusty rings found elsewhere in the solar system.

Backlit view of Uranus's rings

The outer ring is bluish like one of Saturn's outer rings. At least one of these outer rings may be composed of water ice that was knocked off a small moon called Mab.

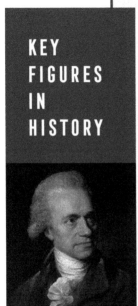

KEY FIGURES IN HISTORY

William Herschel

Not only did **WILLIAM HERSCHEL** *(1738–1822)* discover Uranus, he also contributed to astronomy in many other ways by using telescopes that he constructed himself. He figured out the rotation rate of Mars, found variations in the polar caps on Mars, and discovered Titania and Oberon, moons of Uranus. He also discovered two moons of Saturn. And if that wasn't enough, he discovered the infrared part of the electromagnetic spectrum.

His sister, Caroline Herschel (1750–1848), started assisting him and later became an accomplished astronomer. This was during a time when women astronomers were basically unheard of. Among her many accomplishments, she discovered several comets. She was also the first woman to receive a salary as a scientist and was given several awards and honors for her work.

William's son, John (1792–1871), continued William's astronomical work. He named several moons of Saturn and Uranus and was a founder of the Royal Astronomical Society.

URANUS'S MOONS

As of 2021, Uranus is known to have twenty-seven moons. There are five large moons that are nearly spherical and orbit near the planet's equatorial plane.

The rest of the moons vary in sizes and orbits. Some of the moons between Uranus and the larger moons interact with the rings. They even act as shepherding moons whose nearby gravity keeps rings narrow. Like the rings, the moons of Uranus tend to be dark.

The five large moons are sometimes referred to as the major moons. They are about half water ice and half rock, except the moon Miranda. This smallest moon may have more water ice. All five major moons lack any significant atmosphere.

Whereas most moons in the solar system are named for Greek or Roman mythological figures, the moons of Uranus are named after characters from the plays of William Shakespeare or the poetry of Alexander Pope.

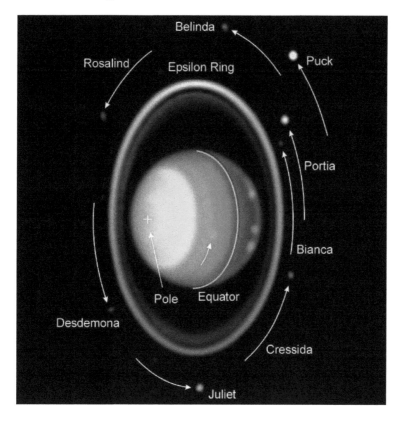

Infrared image of Uranus

What would you think of a planet named George? When astronomer William Herschel discovered what would eventually be named Uranus, he tried to name it after King George III of Great Britain. He planned to name it Georgium Sidus, a Latin phrase meaning George's Star. Not surprisingly, astronomers outside Great Britain were not big fans. A name wasn't agreed upon until decades after the discovery, although the name Uranus had been suggested a year after discovery by the German astronomer Johann Bode (1747–1826).

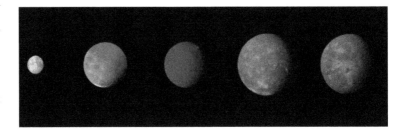

Miranda, Ariel (partial), Umbriel, Titania, Oberon

TITANIA

Titania (tai-TAY-nee-uh) is the largest of Uranus's moons. Although it is the eighth largest moon in the solar system, it is relatively small. It is a little less than one-quarter of the diameter of Earth's Moon, which is the fifth largest in the solar system. Titania is heavily cratered and has other features such as cracks and canyons formed by past activity including faulting of the surface.

OBERON

Whereas Titania is named after the queen of the fairies in Shakespeare's *A Midsummer Night's Dream*, the second-largest and outermost of the five moons is named after Oberon (OH-ber-on), the king of the fairies in the same play. It is heavily cratered

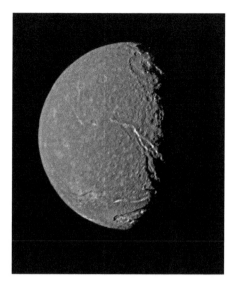

Titania, with craters and canyons

with an ancient surface showing little indication of internal activity.

UMBRIEL

Umbriel (UM-bree-el) also has an ancient surface and is the darkest of the five moons. It does have a bright ring of material in the crater Wunda that is a bit of a mystery. It could be material excavated by an impact, or it could be a deposit of carbon dioxide ice.

ARIEL

Ariel (EH-ree-uhl) is the brightest of the five moons with the youngest overall surface, though likely not very young. It does have significant valleys and ridges crisscrossing the surface, geological activity likely due to tidal heating in the past. *Voyager 2* provided the only close-up views of the moons of Uranus during its high-speed flyby. Because coverage is limited, we only have partial images of Ariel.

MIRANDA

Miranda (mer-AN-duh), the smallest of the five, has the weirdest appearance. Its surface is unlike any other moon in the solar system. It looks like it was pulled apart and then put back together again with sharp boundaries between lines going different directions. One theory to explain this is that an impact broke it apart and it came back together. Currently, another theory favored by many is that upward movement of warmer ice is causing the features through a complex process. Miranda has claim to the highest cliff in the solar system, Verona Rupes, at some 12 miles (20 kilometers) high.

Uranus's moon Miranda

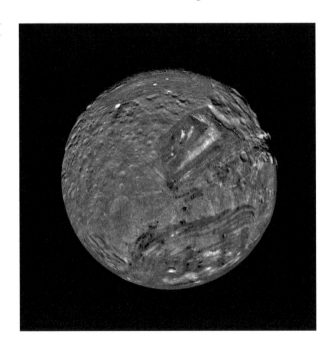

NEPTUNE

DIAMETER: *30,775 miles (49,528 kilometers)*

MASS: *17.1 Earth masses*

AVERAGE DISTANCE FROM THE SUN: *30.0 AU*

KNOWN MOONS: *14*

LENGTH OF DAY: *0.67 Earth day (16.1 hours)*

LENGTH OF YEAR: *163.7 Earth years (59,800 days)*

AVERAGE TEMPERATURE: *-330 degrees Fahrenheit (-200 degrees Celsius)*

Neptune (NEP-toon), a giant planet named after the Roman god of the sea, is the eighth planet from the Sun. Because it is so far from the Sun, it receives only 0.1 percent of the sunlight we receive on Earth. It's cold out there! And it's really far away. If you could drive a car straight from Earth to Neptune, it would take over 5,000 years to get there.

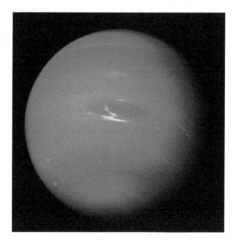

Neptune from Voyager 2

Neptune is blue. It is slightly smaller than Uranus but has slightly more mass. Like Uranus, it is an ice giant. Unlike other planets, Neptune cannot be seen in our sky—it must be viewed through a telescope.

In the 1800s, astronomers realized that something was pulling Uranus off the path of its normal orbit. French mathematician Urbain Le Verrier used that discrepancy to calculate the approximate location of an undiscovered planet. He sent the prediction to German astronomer Johann Galle, who used it to discover Neptune in 1846.

NEPTUNE'S ATMOSPHERE

Voyager 2 is the only spacecraft to ever explore Uranus and Neptune. It flew by Neptune in 1989, revealing that the planet was blue like Uranus but with significant cloud features. Most striking was a storm system the size of Earth, later dubbed the Great Dark Spot. In contrast with Jupiter's Great Red Spot, which is hundreds of years old, the Great Dark Spot disappeared within a few years. In fact, white and dark spots have been seen to come and go since then. This is shown in images from the Hubble Space Telescope and large ground-based telescopes.

The atmosphere of Neptune is similar to Jupiter and Saturn—mostly hydrogen with some helium. But Neptune, along with Uranus, has more methane,

1994 Hubble images showing missing Great Dark Spot

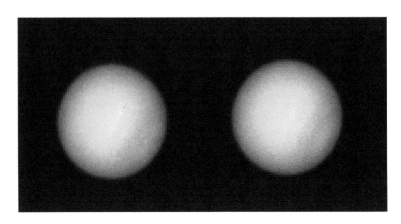

which causes its blue-green color. Neptune is bluer, so there may be something else in its atmosphere affecting its color.

Neptune has the fastest winds ever measured in the solar system at about 1,200 miles per hour (2,000 kilometers per hour). For comparison, Earth's fastest measured wind speeds in a hurricane are about 200 miles per hour (320 kilometers per hour) and about 300 miles per hour (480 kilometers per hour) in a tornado. Without solid surfaces to dissipate energy, high winds are easier to sustain on the giant planets.

FUN FACT

Completing what was known as the Grand Tour, *Voyager 2* launched in 1977 and became the only spacecraft to visit four planets. It flew by Jupiter in 1979, Saturn in 1981, Uranus in 1986, and Neptune in 1989. The spacecraft used the gravity of each planet to help adjust its course to reach the next planet. *Voyager 2* and its sister craft, *Voyager 1*, vastly increased our knowledge of the Jupiter and Saturn systems, including the discovery of moons, rings, and so much more. As of 2021, both spacecraft are still working and leaving the solar system.

*Neptune and
Triton*

NEPTUNE'S STRUCTURE

Neptune, like Uranus, is an ice giant made mostly of water, ammonia, and methane. Below Neptune's atmosphere, there is a large region of water with ammonia and methane existing in a high-pressure fluid form. Deep down, there is a rocky core.

Like the other giant planets, Neptune has a significant magnetic field. Neptune's is tilted about 47 degrees from the spin axis and offset from its center, somewhat similar to Uranus. In both cases, the magnetic field may be generated by the movement of electrically conducting fluids. It's likely some combination of ammonia, water, and methane.

*Interior of
Neptune*

■ *Core
(rock, ice)*

▨ *Mantle (water,
ammonia,
methane ices)*

▨ *Hydrogen,
helium,
methane gas*

Neptune is somewhat higher in mass than Uranus. The entire mass creates higher gravity, which causes its atmosphere to compress more. All this makes Neptune's diameter slightly smaller than Uranus. Neptune is also the densest of the giant planets, with an average density of about 1.6 times the density of liquid water.

Deep inside Neptune, methane breaks apart into carbon and hydrogen. This likely happens in the other giant planets, too. Because the pressure is so high, some scientists have calculated that the carbon can be compressed into diamonds that rain like hail.

NEPTUNE'S RINGS

Before *Voyager 2* was able to get a closer look at Neptune, scientists used telescopic observations to look for the planet's rings. They found material that seemed to be ring arcs, but not a complete ring around the planet. When *Voyager 2* flew by in 1989, it found five distinct but faint rings. The rings are very dark. Like Jupiter's, they're made mostly of dust rather than the ice that makes up the rings of Saturn and Uranus. The outer-most ring does have

Neptune's rings with clumpy arcs

clumpy arcs of material but also has a faint contin-uous ring all the way around. Computer modeling shows that a small moon named Galatea wrangles the arcs into their current positions. The moon is just inward from the ring. In addition to the five main rings, there may be thin, broad rings as well.

Neptune's rings are thought to be relatively young. The main rings are called Galle, Le Verrier, Lassell, Arago, and Adams. They're each named after scientists who were involved in the discovery or early observation of Neptune.

Only a few decades ago, we thought Saturn was the only planet with rings. We've since learned that all the giant planets have ring systems, but they vary greatly.

SPACE IN DAILY LIFE

Most of us rely on weather predictions in our daily life, usually to decide if we need to take an umbrella or grab a jacket. But weather can also be deadly in the form of hurricanes and other large storms.

Our ability to predict the weather and keep us safe has been massively improved by spaceflight. Weather satellites have allowed us to observe dangerous storms and their movements and, more important, issue warnings and evacuations to those who could be in harm's way. The first successful weather satellite launched in 1960. Since then, there have been huge improvements. The way in which we use different wavelengths to study planets is equally important to our weather satellites. For example, visible wavelengths are used to see clouds in the daytime, but infrared measurements let us "see" clouds at night. The same satellites provide insights to phenomena such as forest fires and volcanic eruptions.

NEPTUNE'S MOONS

As of 2021, Neptune is known to have fourteen moons. Triton is the largest by far and is a fascinating world on its own. None of the other thirteen are large enough for their gravity to shape them into spheres. Neptune is named after the Roman god of the sea, whereas its moons are named for lesser sea gods and nymphs in Greek mythology.

Triton was discovered by English astronomer William Lassell in 1846, just seventeen days after Johann Galle discovered Neptune. But because the other moons are so much smaller, it would be over one hundred years before the next moon, Nereid, was discovered.

Neptune's moon Proteus

Records show that various astronomers over the centuries observed Uranus and Neptune without knowing what they were seeing. They assumed what they saw was just another star and noted that in their observations. As the two most distant planets, they have the longest orbits and slowest movement in the solar system. That makes their motion through the sky very slow, which undoubtedly contributed to astronomers not realizing they had found planets. There is evidence that even Galileo recorded Neptune back in 1613 while making some of the first telescopic observations of the sky. And English astronomer John Flamsteed recorded Uranus as a star in a 1690 catalog.

TRITON

Triton is the largest of Neptune's moons, with 99.5 percent of the entire mass orbiting the planet. It's the seventh largest moon in the solar system and the only large moon that orbits retrograde. That means it orbits in the opposite direction of its planet's spin. This is a big clue that tells us it probably did not form with Neptune. Moons that form when the planet forms go in the same direction as the rotation of the planet. Triton is believed to be an object from the Kuiper Belt that was pulled into Neptune's orbit.

Because Triton is so far from the Sun, it is very cold, with surface temperatures around −391 degrees Fahrenheit (−235 degrees Celsius). Its surface is unlike any other in the solar system. Some of Triton's terrain looks like the rind of a cantaloupe. This is why scientists called it cantaloupe terrain.

There are active geysers, which appear to be some combination of liquid nitrogen, methane, and dust. They seem to be triggered when dark material below the surface heats up and breaks through to the surface.

Triton has a very thin nitrogen atmosphere, only 0.0014 percent of the pressure at Earth's surface. In other words, there is barely any pressure, like the edge of space in Earth's atmosphere. Still, Triton's atmosphere has enough wind to blow material from the geysers. In at least some cases, this causes dark wind streaks as the material is deposited elsewhere. *Voyager* images showed one geyser plume shooting up 5 miles (8 kilometers) and drifting 87 miles (140 kilometers) downwind.

When *Voyager 2* flew by Triton, it was flying so fast that it had only enough time and geometry to capture images of 40 percent of the moon's surface. Who knows what some future spacecraft may discover?

Voyager 2 *image of Triton*

CAREERS IN ASTRONOMY

The space industry needs people with many different skills beyond the specialties of scientists, engineers, and astronauts. There is a lot more that happens behind the scenes to make space exploration possible. Space agencies and science organizations have lots of people who work in management, accounting, and law. The space industry is also very dependent on computer support, administrative assistants, facilities personnel, technicians, marketing professionals, fundraisers, and more. These wide-ranging roles can be fun and rewarding. If you're interested in space, no matter what your skills or experience, you probably can find a career that deals with space exploration in some way. You can start getting an idea of job options by searching the Internet. Try looking at the websites of space agencies, aerospace companies, and professional organizations. Go to the Resources section at this back of this book for some links to get you started.

CENTAURS

A centaur (SEN-tor) is a small solar-system body that orbits between Jupiter and Neptune. That's the simple definition, but details vary between different sources. There will continue to be confusion and evolution of terminology as we head even farther out in the solar system, partly because it's so hard to observe objects at those distances. This is especially the case with smaller ones like centaurs.

Most centaurs are thought to be at least some-what icy. If they came closer to the Sun, many would probably be classified as comets. In fact, some are classified as both centaurs *and* comets.

Centaurs change over the course of the object's lifetime. Because they cross the orbits of giant planets, the powerful gravity from these planets eventually changes their orbit. Centaurs could be flung inward, outward, or into other parts of the solar system. Depending on how their orbits change, they may fall into a different category, such as comets. Most of these objects are thought to stay as centaurs for only a period of millions of years. This is short compared to a 4.5-billion-year-old solar system.

No spacecraft has ever vis-ited a centaur because of their distance from Earth and com-petition with other possible planetary missions. As of 2021, about 1,000 have been found, but estimates of the total population are very uncertain. It's possible there are millions of centaurs in the solar system.

Chiron seen from the Hubble Space Telescope

The first centaur was not discovered until 1977. This 125-mile-long (200-kilometer) object was called Chiron and was originally classified as an asteroid. Years later, gas and dust surrounding the object were detected, so it was then classified as a comet. In the 1990s, more of these objects were discovered, and they were named centaurs. The largest centaur dis-covered so far is Chariklo, which is about 155 miles (250 kilometers) in diameter. Amazingly, it was found to have two rings around it.

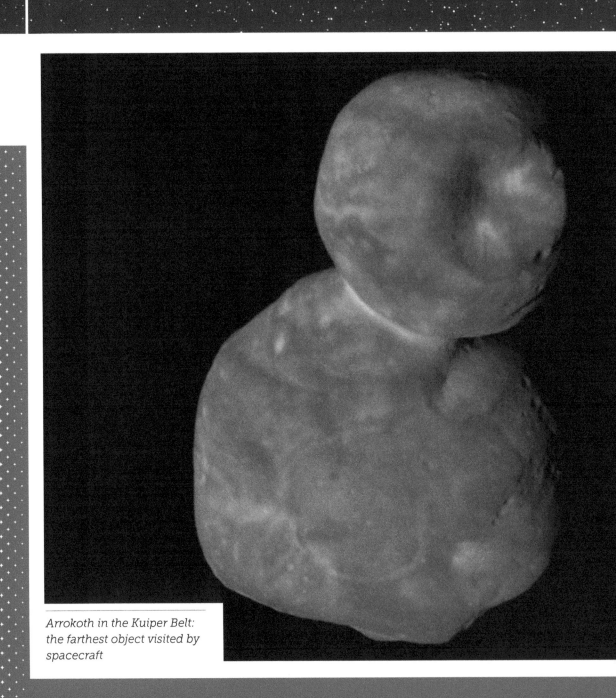

Arrokoth in the Kuiper Belt: the farthest object visited by spacecraft

FOUR

DWARF PLANETS, THE KUIPER BELT, AND BEYOND

Beyond Neptune's orbit are millions of trans-Neptunian (nep-TOON-ee-an) objects (TNOs). These are objects that spend most of their orbit beyond Neptune, the farthest planet in our solar system. Discovering them at that distance is very challenging and requires large telescopes. As of 2021, we know of more than 2,000 TNOs.

TNOs include objects in the Kuiper (KAI-per) Belt, a doughnut-shaped region of icy bodies between 30 AU and 50 AU. There are also scattered disk objects whose orbits extend beyond the Kuiper Belt.

The Kuiper Belt is also home to dwarf planets: Ceres in the asteroid belt and Pluto, Eris, Makemake, and Haumea in the Kuiper Belt. Dwarf planets are large enough to be shaped into rounded spheres by their own gravity. They directly orbit the Sun. But unlike the eight planets of our solar system, they have other things in orbits similar to theirs. Many more dwarf planets will likely be found.

Comets are icy objects that come toward the inner solar system. They give off gas and dust as they travel, which forms the tails they are famous for. Some comets are within Neptune's orbit, whereas others are TNOs. Far, far beyond the Kuiper Belt is the Oort cloud. It is a huge spherical volume of space with cold, dark, icy objects. Some comets come in from the Oort cloud.

PLUTO

DIAMETER: *1,476 miles (2,376 kilometers)*

MASS: *0.0022 Earth masses*

AVERAGE DISTANCE FROM THE SUN: *39.24 AU*

KNOWN MOONS: *5*

LENGTH OF DAY: *6.4 Earth days (153.3 hours)*

LENGTH OF YEAR: *247.9 Earth years (90,560 days)*

AVERAGE TEMPERATURE: *–375 degrees Fahrenheit (–225 degrees Celsius)*

Pluto in true color

The largest dwarf planet, Pluto (PLOO-toh), is a Kuiper Belt object. It spends most of its 248-year orbit far beyond the orbit of Neptune. It goes out to 49 AU and then comes in a little closer than Neptune's orbit at about 30 AU.

Pluto was discovered in 1930 by Clyde Tombaugh at Lowell Observatory in Arizona. He found it by looking for starlike dots that moved from one telescope picture to the next. At the time, Pluto was classified as a planet. In 2006, Pluto was reclassified as a dwarf planet.

Pluto was named after the Roman god of the underworld. The name was given by Venetia Burney, an eleven-year-old English schoolgirl. She suggested it to her grandfather, a former Oxford University librarian. He passed it along to an Oxford astronomy professor who communicated it to Tombaugh.

Pluto has one large moon named Charon (SHAIR-un) that is half the diameter of Pluto. There are at least four much smaller moons.

PLUTO'S ATMOSPHERE AND SURFACE

We got our first detailed look at Pluto when the *New Horizons* space-craft flew by in 2015. It showed a surprisingly complex geology for a frozen world beyond Neptune. There are bright plains made of nitrogen ice along with some carbon monoxide ice. These plains show evidence of the horizontal movement of ices—in other words, glaciers. The plains are relatively young, perhaps less than tens of thousands of years old.

Pluto's icy mountains and plains

Pluto also has older, darker regions. These include mountains made of water ice, some with caps of methane ice. Beneath these ices, there are probably a water ice mantle and a rocky core. Pluto is only about two-thirds the diameter of Earth's moon, so it would stretch only about halfway across the United States.

Pluto's atmosphere is very thin and made primarily of nitrogen, with some methane and carbon monoxide. At the time of the *New Horizons* flyby, the atmosphere was very thin, almost like it is high up in the Earth's atmosphere at the edge of space. As Pluto moves away from the Sun in its orbit, the atmosphere

Pluto's moon Charon

begins to freeze and therefore becomes even thinner.

Pluto and its moon Charon are both tidally locked to the other. This means the same side of Pluto always faces the same side of Charon. So, if you were on the other side of Pluto, you'd never see Charon. Thus, a day on Pluto is the same duration as a day on Charon—about 6.5 Earth days.

FUN FACT

New Horizons was the fastest spacecraft ever launched at the time, but it still took 9.5 years to reach distant Pluto. When it flew past Pluto in 2015, it was about three million miles (five million kilometers) from Earth and traveling tens of thousands of miles per hour. Because it was 4.5 light-hours away, it took 4.5 hours for radio commands or data to go one way. Receiving a signal on Earth and then sending back a command would take at least nine hours. From Earth, we cannot actively control the spacecraft during a short flyby. These encounters are completely preplanned and run by the onboard computers.

OTHER DWARF PLANETS

Besides Pluto, there are three other known dwarf planets beyond Neptune: Eris, Makemake, and Haumea. Very little is known about these objects because they are so far away and have not been visited by spacecraft. They appear as dots even in powerful telescope images.

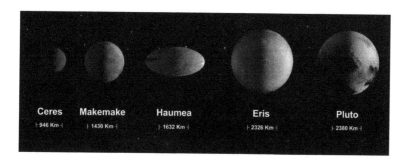

Ceres   Makemake   Haumea   Eris   Pluto
⊢ 946 Km ⊣ ⊢ 1430 Km ⊣ ⊢ 1632 Km ⊣ ⊢ 2326 Km ⊣ ⊢ 2380 Km ⊣

Illustration of dwarf planet sizes

ERIS

Eris (AIR-iss) has the most mass of any known dwarf planet. It is about a third more massive than Pluto but slightly smaller in diameter. This scattered disk object has a 557-year orbit around the Sun. It comes in as close as 38 AU and

Eris and its moon, Dysnomia

goes out as far as 98 AU. Its orbit takes it high above and then farther below the plane of the other planets' orbits. Eris is known to have one moon, Dysnomia.

MAKEMAKE

Makemake (MAH-kay-MAH-kay), like Eris, was discovered in 2005. Its discovery contributed to the debate over the definition of a planet. Although Makemake is much smaller than Pluto or Eris, it is still large enough to be shaped into a round sphere by its gravity. It takes 305 years to go around the Sun and has an average distance of about 48 AU. Makemake is named after the Rapa Nui fertility god.

HAUMEA

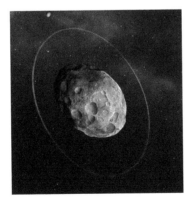

Illustration of Haumea and its ring

Haumea (how-MAY-ah) is one of the fastest rotating objects in the solar system, especially for such a small object. It is only several hundred miles in diameter. Haumea rotates in four hours, which has caused it to elongate into a football shape. It has two known moons and even has rings. Its year is 285 Earth years long, and its average distance from the Sun is 43 AU. Haumea is named after the Hawaiian fertility goddess.

THE KUIPER BELT

The doughnut-shaped region between 30 AU and about 50 AU from the Sun is referred to as the Kuiper Belt. It is named after Gerard Kuiper, a Dutch American planetary scientist. The dwarf planets, comets, and other material found in this region are called Kuiper Belt objects.

Another group of objects that can be found within the Kuiper Belt are known as scattered disc objects. Compared to Kuiper Belt objects, they go farther out. They're often at much higher angles compared to the plane of the other planets' orbits. Scattered disc objects are sometimes referred to as part of the Kuiper Belt and sometimes not. As of 2021, we're still in the early phases of discovering objects beyond Neptune, so terminology is evolving and not always consistent.

Kuiper Belt objects and scattered disc objects are thought to be the icy leftovers from when planets formed.

COMETS

Comets are dirty snowball objects that venture into the inner solar system from the outer solar system. Some spend time in the Kuiper Belt. When a comet approaches the Sun, the ices warm up and turn from a solid to a gas. This forms a cloud of gas and dust surrounding the comet referred to as the coma.

Effects of the Sun push the coma material out in two tails. One tail is dusty and white, whereas the other often appears blue or green. The tails always stretch out opposite the direction of the Sun. Thus, when they head away from the Sun, their tails are in front, not trailing behind.

Comet with its tails

Sometimes there are comets visible in the night sky with binoculars, and occasionally you can see one with just your eyes. They're usually visible for weeks, moving very slowly across the sky from one night to the next.

Comet 67P with dust and gas coming off

There are two categories of comets. Short-period comets like Halley's Comet take 200 years or less to orbit the Sun. The orbit of long-period comets ranges from 201 years to hundreds of thousands of years. Their orbits take them thousands of AU away from the Sun.

What else is out there? We have only begun to scratch the surface of the solar system beyond Neptune. Although we've discovered thousands of objects, there are likely at least many millions. How many more will we discover in the coming decades? What will they be like? How many will be dwarf planets? There is even the possibility of a planet-size object in the more distant reaches of the solar system.

Even in the inner solar system, only a fraction of the asteroids have been found. Whether they're in the asteroid belt or among the near-Earth asteroids, they could pose threats to our planet. The exciting thing is that technology keeps advancing. This will help us learn more so we can try to uncover these mysteries. Enormous ground-based telescopes and highly capable space telescopes will be going online in the coming years. You can look forward to a lot of discoveries in your lifetime.

HYPOTHETICAL PLANET X

In the 1800s, scientists used the orbit of Uranus to predict the location of an undiscovered, farther-out planet. They found what would come to be known as Neptune very near that location.

More recently, some scientists have theorized the existence of another planet far out in the solar system.

They found evidence by calculating the orbits for certain Kuiper Belt objects and scattered disc objects. This hypothetical planet has been dubbed Planet 9. It is thought to be about 400 AU from the Sun, which is more than thirteen times farther than Neptune.

The calculated mass and size of Planet 9 are midway between those of Earth and Neptune. This would put it in a category called a super-Earth. This is a size that has not been discovered in our solar system so far but is very common among planets outside our solar system that orbit other stars.

Planet 9 and cluster of orbits (purple)

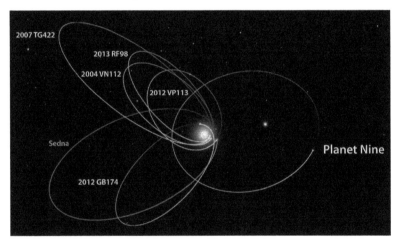

THE OORT CLOUD

The Oort (pronounced ORT) cloud contains the most distant objects in our solar system. It was first theorized by Dutch astronomer Jan Oort in 1950, who was trying to solve the mystery of where long-period comets come from.

The Oort cloud is a spherical collection of icy bodies. The inner edge is thought to be located 2,000 AU to 5,000 AU from the Sun, compared to

Neptune at 30 AU. The outer edge is thought to be somewhere between 10,000 AU and 100,000 AU. That's one-third of the way to the nearest star. These distances are calculated by determining the orbits of comets that enter the inner solar system.

For reference, the *Voyager 1* spacecraft is the farthest spacecraft from Earth and traveling the fastest of any spacecraft leaving the solar system. It travels about 1 million miles per day (1.6 million kilometers per day). It won't even enter the Oort cloud for about 300 years and won't exit for as much as 30,000 years.

Objects likely did not form in the Oort cloud but closer to the Sun. They were later thrown out to the Oort cloud by the gravity of the giant planets.

The Oort cloud is heavily influenced by the gravity of other stars as well as the galaxy. Those interactions may dislodge objects and send them into the inner solar system as long-period comets.

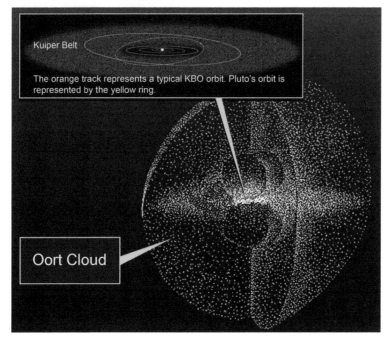

Kuiper Belt and Oort cloud

Parker Solar Probe

FIVE

For most of human history, people explored space just by looking up at the sky with their eyes. But in the past few centuries, we have vastly improved the capability to explore space from the ground. We have even gone to space. In this chapter, we will explore important historical achievements and technological developments, including missions to different parts of the solar system. Then it's time for you to explore space directly! We'll learn about backyard astronomy with different tips, tricks, and techniques for stargazing sessions. Find out the tools you'll need and all the different things you'll be able to see from your own home.

THE HISTORY OF STUDYING SPACE

Most cultures throughout history have observed the sky. But almost none interpreted the sky's information correctly when it came to the solar system and the universe. The Sun, the Moon, and the stars all looked as if they were moving, whereas the Earth looked as if it weren't. Because of this, people thought that Earth was the center of the universe with everything else revolving around it. This idea is known as the geo-centric model of the universe. It was popularized in the second century CE by the Roman mathematician Ptolemy, and people went along with it. His ideas dominated for more than 1,300 years!

There is at least one ancient exception. In the fourth century BCE, Greek astronomer Aristarchus theorized that the Earth rotates on its axis and moves around the Sun. This was hundreds of years before Ptolemy and 1,800 years before the Sun-centered solar system became generally accepted. In fact, Copernicus, the person who would restart thinking about the Sun-centered universe, was aware of and presumably influenced by the thinking of Aristarchus.

A lot has happened since then, including the following four huge developments and discoveries in our understanding of the solar system. We'll look at the Copernican model of the universe, laws of motion, the electromagnetic spectrum and spectros-copy, and exoplanets.

COPERNICAN MODEL OF THE UNIVERSE

In 1543, Polish mathematician Nicolaus Copernicus published the idea that everything revolves around the Sun, not the Earth. His theory correctly included the rotation of the Earth and the movement of the planets in the correct order around the Sun. It also explained various observations, including retrograde motion of planets. This is when planets appear to move backward in the sky when they lap Earth or when Earth laps them in orbit.

He got some things wrong, but the basics of his theory would slowly come to be accepted in the following centuries as others built upon his work.

In the couple hundred years that immediately followed his publication, however, the theory was

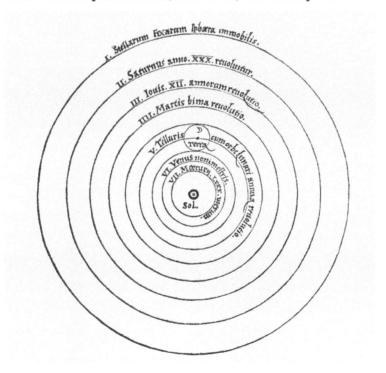

Copernicus's original model with circular orbits

extremely controversial. Some of the religions of the world opposed the concept of not putting Earth at the center of everything. It conflicted with their belief systems and how they understood the world.

LAWS OF MOTION AND IMPROVED SOLAR SYSTEM MODELS

After Copernicus, other people provided more evidence that the planets revolved around the Sun. In the early 1600s, Galileo was the first to use a telescope to study the sky. He made key observations that were consistent with the Earth's orbit around the Sun. (For more info on Galileo, see page 32.)

Around the same time, German astronomer Johannes Kepler came up with laws of motion that described and correctly predicted the way planets moved around the Sun. His key breakthrough was realizing the planets orbit in ellipses. This was in contrast to the idea that planets each orbited the Sun in a large perfect circle, which had been proposed by Copernicus.

In the late 1600s, English physicist Isaac Newton developed equations that described gravity. He also recognized that gravity was holding the planets in their orbits around the Sun. His concept of gravity explained why Kepler's laws were true.

THE ELECTROMAGNETIC SPECTRUM AND SPECTROSCOPY

In the 1800s, scientists discovered the electromagnetic spectrum. Different wavelengths on the spectrum tell us different things about planetary objects and stars. For example, ultraviolet and X-ray observations allow us to see features in the Sun's atmosphere that we wouldn't see otherwise. Infrared allows us to measure the temperature of planets from a distance. It's like a really long-range thermometer.

A related discovery was spectroscopy. White light is made up of all the colors of the rainbow. In the 1800s, German physicist Joseph von Fraunhofer split white light coming from the Sun into its component colors, or wavelengths. He found black lines at certain wavelengths. When he compared the lines with ones found in laboratory studies of hydrogen, he saw that they matched. This showed hydrogen was part of what made up the Sun. These spectral lines, which occur in all wavelengths, are different for different materials. Just as fingerprints can identify a person, spectral lines can be used to identify what things are made of.

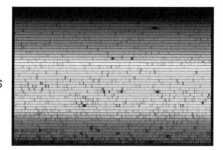

Solar spectrum showing black spectral lines

EXOPLANETS

Exoplanets are planets that orbit stars other than the Sun. They were first discovered in the 1990s. Since that time, thousands of exoplanets have been found, mostly by dedicated space telescopes. These discoveries have reshaped the way we think about our solar system.

Finding exoplanets is very challenging because they are very dim compared to the stars they orbit. Very few have been directly imaged. They have

Exoplanet (blue dot lower left)

mostly been discovered in one of two ways: by looking for the tiny dip in light coming from the star when a planet passes in front or by looking at the wobble of a star due to the gravity of a planet.

We have found that different solar systems vary significantly. For example, there are Jupiter-size gas giants that orbit very close to their stars. We are only at the beginning of this exciting field of study.

FUN FACT

The spectrum of the Sun is how the element helium was discovered. Helium is what makes party balloons float. In 1868, an unknown spectral line was found in the spectrum of the Sun. It wasn't until 1881 that this spectral line was observed on Earth. It was seen in gas from a volcanic eruption. Then it wasn't until 1895 that helium would be isolated in a laboratory. Thanks to spectroscopy, helium was discovered on the Sun before it was ever discovered on Earth. The name *helium* comes from *helios*, the Greek word for the Sun.

THE DEVELOPMENT OF SPACE PROGRAM TECHNOLOGY

Technology has been crucial to the development of our understanding of the solar system. Everything in space is very far away, so humans were very limited in their ability to study space. It wasn't until the Renaissance in the fifteenth, sixteenth, and seventeenth centuries that astronomy tools like telescopes were invented. Over time, we have developed better and better telescopes and even developed spacecraft that go out into space and explore the solar system directly.

The four technological advancements discussed here—telescopes, film and detectors, rockets, and computers—have revolutionized the way we think about the solar system. But these are only a few of many groundbreaking inventions, and technology continues to improve. People are building more sensitive detectors, making miniature versions of various scientific instruments so they can fly in spacecraft, and so much more. The future looks bright, and you can play a part in the next great technological or scientific discoveries!

Space shuttle astronauts work on the Hubble Space Telescope

TELESCOPES

Before the invention of the telescope, most objects in the night sky looked like tiny dots. Telescopes use things like lenses and mirrors to make objects appear larger as well as gather more light from dim objects.

Telescopes got larger over the centuries, gathering more light and magnifying more. In recent times, space telescopes have made observations without the interference of the atmosphere. The Hubble Space Telescope launched in 1990 and is still operating successfully as of 2021. Just as Galileo's first telescope did, the Hubble telescope has made incredible dis-coveries and shaped theories of the universe. It has discovered moons, allowed regular monitoring of the farthest planets, and provided some of our best images of dwarf planets in the outer solar system.

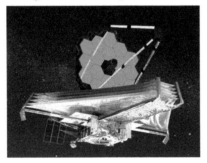

Artist's concept of the James Webb Space Telescope

The James Webb Space Telescope launched in 2021. Much larger than Hubble, it will see even farther with more detail and more wavelengths than Hubble.

FILM AND DETECTORS

For more than 200 years after the invention of the telescope in 1608, the only detector that was used was the human eye. Records were only as accurate as the observer who made them.

The invention of photographic glass plates, the precursor to film, enabled more reliable and detailed science. Images showed dimmer objects and provided accurate long-term records. Pluto was found by comparing two photographic plates taken six days apart and looking for any faint objects that moved. Pictures over time have shown the gradual shrinking of Jupiter's Great Red Spot.

Another leap forward was the invention of digital detectors, like charge-coupled devices (CCDs) and CMOS. They began getting heavy use in astronomy in the 1980s. These detectors are much more sensitive and more accurate than film. Now, when you take a selfie with a phone camera, you are using a commercial version of one of these detectors.

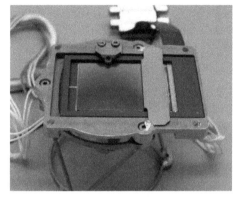

Charge-coupled device (CCD) used in Curiosity

ROCKETS

Rockets are used to send spacecraft into space. They work by burning fuel, which creates hot gas that exits through a nozzle at the back of the rocket. The gas blasts out at high speeds, causing the rocket to move forward.

Russian Soyuz *rocket carrying three people*

The first rockets date back to China in the thirteenth century. They were used as fireworks and military weapons. The first modern rockets were developed by Robert Goddard in the United States in the 1920s using liquid fuel.

During World War II, the Germans developed the V-2 supersonic rocket as one of their weapons. At the end of the war, the Americans and the Soviets captured leaders of the German rocket program and used them in their own programs. Rocket development was very rapid in the 1950s and 1960s, culminating in the United States developing the most powerful rocket ever used, the *Saturn V*. This is the rocket that sent humans to the Moon.

COMPUTERS

Computers have enabled huge leaps forward in space studies and exploration. When humans began to take flight in the 1950s, computers were so big that they filled entire rooms. Now cell phones have more powerful computers in them than any of the computers used in the first decades of spaceflight.

Apollo Guidance Computer (left) and input

Because planets and other objects in the solar system are so far away, our communication takes minutes to hours to reach them—even when it travels at the speed of light—so computers are programmed in advance to control planetary flybys and even landings. Mars rovers have computers that are given instructions to carry out, but they can make decisions about avoiding hazards while driving.

In science, computers enable everything from storing and processing images to modeling planetary processes. The engineering of everything from telescopes to spacecraft to scientific instruments is now carried out and improved using computers.

During the beginning of NASA's space program, computers were enormous and not as advanced as they are today. Groups of female mathematicians were hired to act as human computers. They computed incredibly complex things using only basic calculators and their own mathematical capabilities. They figured out spacecraft trajectories and calculated adjustments during a spacecraft's flight.

Among these pioneers were the Black women who were the focus of the 2016 movie *Hidden Figures*. **DOROTHY VAUGHAN, KATHERINE JOHNSON, AND MARY JACKSON** were human computers at Langley Research Center in the 1950s. The law at that time required them to work in a segregated group, which meant they were separated from their white colleagues. Despite this prejudice, they all went on to have very successful NASA careers. Jackson became NASA's first female African American engineer in 1958. Johnson would go on to calculate trajectories for the first American human spaceflights. Vaughan was the first Black woman to supervise a group at Langley.

KEY FIGURES IN HISTORY

Mary W. Jackson

SPACE PROGRAMS

The first space programs came from the United States and the Soviet Union during the Cold War era of the mid-twentieth century. The two countries competed to lead the way in space exploration. Eventually, many other countries developed Earth satellites, and several pursued deep space explorations to the Moon or beyond.

In 1957, the Soviet Union launched *Sputnik*. It was the first satellite to enter space and orbit Earth. A year later, the United States formed the National Aeronautics and Space Administration (NASA). NASA carries out government space exploration and performs aeronautical and space research. It remains the largest space agency in the world. In space, NASA carries out deep space robotic exploration and studies, monitors Earth from space, and puts humans in space.

The Soviet, and later Russian, space programs carried out planetary exploration and have had robust human space programs. They completed successful missions to Venus in the 1970s and 1980s. The Russian space agency is now called Roscosmos. It and

Crew on the International Space Station

the United States are lead partners on the International Space Station (ISS).

The European Space Agency (ESA) is the joint space agency for twenty-two countries in Europe. It has had several successful planetary missions, carries out Earth research, and has space telescopes. ESA has partnered with NASA several times and is a partnering agency of the ISS.

The Japanese space agency, JAXA, carries out Earth observation and has space telescopes. It is a partner in the ISS, providing special cargo spacecraft. JAXA has sent spacecraft to near-Earth asteroids to collect samples.

Other nations around the world have active space agencies. The Canadian Space Agency is the other partner on the ISS. The Indian Space Research Organization (ISRO) has flown planetary missions as well as missions that orbit Earth. China has become very active in planetary exploration in recent years. The country has its own human space program that includes small space stations.

SATELLITES

A satellite is an object that orbits another object. Moons are an example of natural satellites, but there are also artificial satellites, which are made and sent into space by humans.

On October 4, 1957, the Soviet Union launched the world's first artificial satellite. It was named *Sputnik 1* and looked like an oversized shiny basketball with four radio antennas. It was basic by today's standards but succeeded in demonstrating the ability to launch an object into space and to receive communications from it. The satellite also helped us learn more about the density of Earth's upper atmosphere. The United States launched its first satellite, *Explorer 1*, a few months later. Both countries had rocket failures and other difficulties before they were able to successfully fly a satellite.

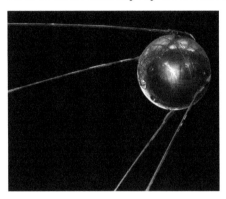

Replica of Sputnik 1

More advanced satellites have since launched over the years. We now have many thousands of operating satellites that perform various functions, including ones that affect our everyday lives. Some satellites provide us with communication services like TV and Internet. Global positioning satellites enable maps on a phone or computer that tell you where you are at any given moment. Other satellites carry out research studying the Earth.

MISSIONS TO THE MOON

More than one hundred missions to the Moon have been attempted. As the closest natural object beyond Earth, it was the focus of early space exploration.

There were many failures by the Soviets and the Americans in the early years. The Soviets had a major milestone with the *Luna 3* spacecraft in 1959. It gave us the first views of the Moon's far side. Although the pictures were crude, they were enough to show us that there are fewer mare on the far side than on the near side. The mare are the dark regions we see when we look up at the Moon.

Both countries wanted to be the first to put a human on the Moon. They mapped the Moon and learned as much as they could before sending humans there. America's *Lunar Orbiter* missions from 1966 to 1967 were particularly successful. The spacecraft gave us our first global coverage of the Moon in any detail. *Lunar Orbiter* images helped people select the landing site for the later Apollo human missions. The United States also landed robotic *Surveyor* spacecraft on the surface, which demonstrated safe landing was possible.

In December 1968, *Apollo 8* sent humans around the Moon. *Apollo 11* landed the first humans on the Moon on July 20, 1969. Neil Armstrong and Buzz Aldrin were the first people to ever walk on another world. Over the next several years, five more Apollo missions would land on the Moon and explore more complex geological environments. The final three missions carried lunar rovers, which were small open cars that astronauts drove on the Moon. Hundreds of pounds of lunar rocks and dirt were brought back by the astronauts, which helped us learn even more about the Moon.

Astronaut Buzz Aldrin on the Moon

There have been numerous highly successful robotic missions to the Moon since Apollo. Among their discoveries is the presence of water ice in lunar craters. Many other countries' space agencies have begun planetary exploration to the Moon. These include Japan, India, and China as well as the European Space Agency. The United

Astronaut visits Surveyor 3 lander

States has continued to explore the Moon over the years. More recently, the *Lunar Reconnaissance Orbiter* began orbiting in 2009 and is giving us our highest-resolution images of the surface. It also provides thermal maps and numerous types of data that help us understand the Moon as a whole.

MISSIONS TO MARS

Over the years, spacecraft have attempted to explore Mars. Although many have succeeded, many have failed.

The first three U.S. trips to Mars were flyby missions in the late 1960s. The spacecraft launched were *Mariner 4*, *Mariner 6*, and *Mariner 7*. They returned grainy images that looked very much like the Moon, showing lots of craters and not much varied geology. They happened to all fly by the heavily cratered southern highlands. Then *Mariner 9* went into orbit in 1971. It had to wait out a global dust storm, but when the dust cleared, it provided amazing images. We finally saw the diverse Martian geology that we know today, including the largest canyon system in the solar system, Valles Marineris.

The *Viking* spacecraft program ran from 1975 to 1982. It consisted of two orbiters and two landers. The landers were the first successful landers on Mars. The orbiters would vastly improve upon the imagery and other data of *Mariner 9*. The landers were designed to test for signs of current microbial life, which they did not find.

There have been working U.S. orbiters on Mars since *Mars Global Surveyor* went into orbit in 1997. U.S. orbiters have been joined by orbiters from Europe, India, China, and the United Arab Emirates.

Several U.S. rovers have explored local areas of interest on the surface of Mars. The first was a small rover named *Sojourner* that landed in 1997. The rovers since then have been *Spirit* and *Opportunity*, which both landed in 2004, and the *Curiosity* rover of 2012. More recently, the car-size *Perseverance* rover landed in 2021. It carried a small helicopter called *Ingenuity*, which successfully demonstrated flying on Mars. A Chinese rover, *Zhurong*, also landed in 2021.

Sojourner,
*the first
Mars rover*

MISSIONS TO THE SUN

The first missions related to the Sun, as well as several of the most recent ones, involve telescopes. These powerful instruments are able to see in wavelength regions blocked by the atmosphere, including the extreme ultraviolet and X-ray.

One example orbiting Earth is NASA's Solar Dynamics Observatory (SDO). Launched in 2010, SDO provides nearly constant imaging of the Sun at many wavelengths. This has been an important tool for studying different layers of the Sun's atmosphere as well as phenomena like sunspots and solar flares. We also now have a detailed record of the solar cycle. This is an eleven-year cycle experienced by the Sun, in which storm activity reaches a climax and settles back down before starting over again.

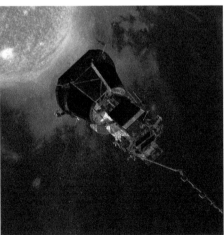

Artist's concept of the Parker Solar Probe

Several spacecraft operate at the Earth-Sun Lagrange point called L1, the gravitational balance point between the Earth and the Sun. L1 is about 1 million miles (1.6 million kilometers) from the Earth. One example is the *Solar and Heliospheric Observatory* spacecraft launched in 1995 and still working as of 2021. In addition to long-term observations of the Sun at several wavelengths, it has instruments to measure the solar wind at L1.

This provides warning of solar storms before they impact the Earth.

A small number of missions have tried to get closer to the Sun, which of course is an enormous challenge because of the incredibly hot environment. In 2018, the NASA's *Parker Solar Probe* set the record for the closest spacecraft to the Sun. In 2021, it got closer and flew through the Sun's corona, which is in the upper reaches of the solar atmosphere. The space probe is designed to measure magnetic fields and the corona. It is also designed to help us understand more about the transfer of energy to the solar wind.

FUN FACT

The *Parker Solar Probe* has not only set records as the closest spacecraft to the Sun, it has also set records as the fastest spacecraft relative to the Sun. The spacecraft goes the fastest at the periapse, the closest point in its orbit to the Sun. As it gets closer to the Sun, the Sun's gravity pulls harder and accelerates the spacecraft. The *Parker Solar Probe* is designed to reach 119 miles *per second* (192 kilometers per second). If it flew across the continental United States at that speed, it would cross the entire country in less than 24 seconds!

MISSIONS TO THE INNER SOLAR SYSTEM BODIES

For more than thirty years, we knew what only half of Mercury looked like based upon the NASA *Mariner 10* flybys in 1974 and 1975. NASA's *MESSENGER* spacecraft filled in the rest of the Mercury map, starting with flybys in 2008 before orbiting in 2011.

Venus has been the focus of missions since the early days of planetary exploration in the 1960s. The U.S. *Magellan* mission launched in 1990, carrying a powerful radar that was used to map the surface through its cloudy atmosphere. It gave us a thorough topography map of the surface, showing Venus's extensive plains and its highland regions. It also showed far fewer than the expected number of craters. This led to the realization that much of Venus's surface was resurfaced hundreds of millions of years ago.

There have been many asteroid missions, including missions to collect samples in the 2010s and 2020s. The first spacecraft to orbit an asteroid was NASA's *NEAR Shoemaker*. It arrived at the 21-mile-long (34-kilometer-long) asteroid Eros. The spacecraft was designed as an orbiter, not a lander. But when the spacecraft was about to run out of fuel, it nonetheless was landed successfully on the surface, making it the first spacecraft to land on an asteroid.

A small number of missions have gone to comets while they were in the inner solar system. One particularly unusual mission was Deep Impact. In 2005, NASA's *Deep Impact* spacecraft purposely slammed a 1,700-pound (800-kilogram) ball of copper into the comet Tempel 1. The goal was to study the material that was ejected. When the spray of material from the impact turned out to be even bigger than expected, we captured spectacular images of the material flying out.

Tempel 1, struck by Deep Impact's spacecraft

MISSIONS TO THE OUTER SOLAR SYSTEM BODIES

Relatively few spacecraft have explored the outer solar system. In addition to being enormously far away, there is far less sunlight available to power the spacecraft. All spacecraft that have gone beyond Jupiter have needed nuclear power sources, with more recent Jupiter spacecraft having enormous solar panels.

The two NASA *Voyager* spacecraft launched in 1977 played an important role in our understanding of the outer solar system. Not only did they study the planets, but they also revealed new information about the larger moons of these planets. *Voyager 1* explored Jupiter and Saturn. *Voyager 2* explored both planets and then went on to be the only spacecraft to encounter Uranus and Neptune. Both *Voyager* spacecraft were still communicating with Earth as of 2021 and are well beyond 100 AU from the Sun.

After the flyby missions came orbiters. The NASA *Galileo* spacecraft orbited Jupiter in the 1990s and released a probe into its atmosphere. The probe was able to tell us more about the composition of Jupiter's atmosphere. The orbiter passed by the large moons several times, providing major insights into the Galilean moons.

Data collected by the spacecraft implied that Europa had a liquid-water ocean under its surface.

The *Cassini-Huygens* mission was a joint endeavor by NASA, the European Space Agency, and Italy's space agency. It involved two spacecraft, which arrived at Saturn in 2004. The *Huygens* spacecraft descended into Titan's thick atmosphere and parachuted down to the surface. *Cassini* orbited Saturn until 2017, when it was intentionally crashed into Saturn. It was almost the size of a school bus, which is huge for a planetary spacecraft. Its studies of

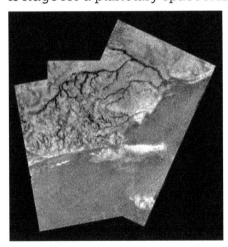

Titan's methane-cut river channels

Saturn, its moons, and its rings taught us many things about the system. Major discoveries included liquid lakes of methane and ethane on Titan and a subsurface liquid-water ocean with active geysers on Enceladus.

MISSIONS TO THE DWARF PLANETS AND KUIPER BELT

Only two missions have ever visited dwarf planets, and only one has visited objects in the Kuiper Belt. *Dawn* launched in 2007 and was the first mission to orbit two different bodies that were not the Earth. In 2011, it orbited the very large Vesta asteroid. Vesta has a diameter of 326 miles (525 kilometers). *Dawn* discovered that the asteroid had a huge impact basin compared to its size. It determined that certain classes of meteorites on Earth came from that impact basin. *Dawn* left Vesta's orbit and went to the dwarf planet Ceres in 2015. Ceres was found to be more complex and unique than expected.

New Horizons launched in 2006 and headed for Pluto. The spacecraft did studies of the Jupiter system as it flew by in 2007. In 2015, it flew through the Pluto system. This gave us our first and only close-up views of this distant dwarf planet and its moons. Pluto was full of surprises and more complexity than people could have predicted. There were mountains, plains, exotic ices, glacial flow, and variability across the surface. *New Horizons* also provided data on Pluto's large moon Charon. One thing it found was a large reddish-brown area. This turned out to be material that had come over from Pluto's atmosphere.

In 2019, *New Horizons* did a flyby of Arrokoth. This is another Kuiper Belt object, and it's the only other one we have detailed

Artist's impression of New Horizons *spacecraft*

information about. Arrokoth was discovered to be a contact binary. This is a small solar system body that consists of two objects. The objects used to be separated until they gravitated toward each other. When they connected in a slow collision, they became a contact binary.

SPACE STATIONS

Early astronauts had to live in their small spacecraft while they visited space. In the 1970s, the Soviets and Americans started using space stations. These large spacecraft are living and working quarters for astronauts, where they can stay for longer periods of time with more room and capabilities.

In 1998, the International Space Station (ISS) began construction in space. The ISS has huge solar arrays and multiple modules that cover an area the size of a football field. To build the station in space, pieces were brought up over many years and assembled by astronauts.

Rotating shifts of people have been on board the space station since November 2000. Astronauts launch on smaller spacecraft, which then dock with the ISS. There are usually around six people on board, and they typically stay for several months.

Astronauts carry out a wide variety of science experiments on the ISS. They've grown crystals, seen the response of plants in space, performed medical tests on themselves to evaluate the effects of long-term space travel on humans, and much more. Besides working, astronauts carry out everyday chores that are modified for space. To stop

The 1970s Skylab space station

them floating around when they exercise, astronauts use a treadmill with straps that hold them down. Their sleeping bags are attached to a wall for the same reason. They eat nutritious food, but they can't sprinkle salt or pepper—it could fly away and get into the equipment. Dirty laundry? That is often sent off with used cargo ships that burn up in the Earth's atmosphere.

SPACE IN DAILY LIFE

Why do we get sunburns? The Sun does indeed cause this painful skin reaction, but visible light is not the main culprit. It's ultraviolet light, which carries more energy than visible light. Sunscreen helps absorb the dangerous UV or reflects it. Without the Earth's atmosphere, sunburns would be more severe and occur much faster, and skin cancer would happen more often. Shorter-wavelength ultraviolet light, which has higher energies, is absorbed by the upper atmosphere. You may have heard of the importance of the ozone layer in this process. Ozone is made up of molecules with three oxygen atoms rather than the usual two. It interacts with the ultraviolet, absorbing it and preventing it from reaching the surface. The ozone layer is Earth's own natural sunscreen! The atmosphere also blocks out the Sun's X-rays and gamma rays. These wavelengths have even higher energies that would be significantly more damaging to humans.

INTERNATIONAL SPACE LAW

Space law refers to the laws that govern space-related activities. There are national laws, and there are international treaties. Any agreement among the countries of the world regarding law is complicated, and space law is no exception.

There have been a handful of treaties regarding space law. One of the first and most important is the Outer Space Treaty, which was put into force in 1967. More than one hundred countries signed this treaty, including all major nations with space programs. The treaty covers lots of things, including the prohibition of nuclear weapons in space and ensuring that space can be explored and used by all countries. There are also treaty points that prohibit a country from claiming outer space or a planetary body as their own.

International discussion of space law is carried out in part by the United Nations Committee on the Peaceful Uses of Outer Space (COPUOS). COPUOS has a subcommittee specifically dedicated to space law. Recent developments in space will have a continuing impact on space laws. This includes people going into space as tourists rather than just professional astronauts. There are also complications related to the possibility of mining asteroids and other bodies in space for metals and other resources.

BACKYARD ASTRONOMY

Looking at the night sky is really fun! Amateur astronomy is a popular and accessible hobby that anyone can enjoy.

You don't need a fancy telescope to begin exploring space. With just your eyes, you can get familiar with the sky. Then, if you wish, you can move into binoculars and telescopes. Some amateur astronomers develop very advanced telescope setups and even contribute important observations to science. Amateur observations of near-Earth asteroids help track them or measure properties such as spin rate. They can determine whether we are seeing one asteroid or a pair of asteroids orbiting each other. Sometimes, amateur astronomers have even discovered a new asteroid.

Amateur astronomers

Read on for stargazing tips, astronomy gear, and more. If this sparks your interest, dig deeper by going to the Resources section at the end of the book.

STARGAZING

Looking at the night sky is easy, but it helps to know some basics that will help you see more things and see them better. Here are some tips, whether you're using telescopes, binoculars, or just your eyes.

Avoid cloudy skies. Use weather predictions to choose clear nights.

Avoid bright lights. Bright stars and planets are visible within most cities, but light pollution from artificial outdoor lights will prevent you from seeing much else.

Plan for the Moon. Look online to find the times that the Moon rises and sets on any given day.

Give your eyes many minutes to adjust to the dark. Avoid phone screens and flashlights unless they are in a dim red-light mode.

Know where and when to look to see a particular object. The night sky appears to move every night, and the objects that are visible change during the course of a year.

ASTRONOMY GEAR

All you need to become an astronomer is yourself, your curiosity, and a lack of clouds. But various gear will add to your experience.

Something to know where different objects are. Examples are a sky chart, a planisphere (see the following section), and a night sky phone app, which you should use in night vision mode.

Red flashlight or flashlight covered in red cellophane so you don't ruin your night vision.

Binoculars are easier to use and have a wider field of view than telescopes, making them good tools for observing the night sky.

Telescopes come in three basic styles. Reflecting telescopes use mirrors, refracting telescopes use lenses, and compound or catadioptric telescopes use lenses and mirrors. In general, a larger primary mirror or main lens to gather more light is better. Go online or find inspiration from the Resources section to learn more about shopping for a telescope.

Refractor telescope

Reflecting telescope

Compound telescope

PLANISPHERES AND NIGHT SKY SOFTWARE

Because of the rotation and orbit of the Earth, the night sky changes. How do you know where to look at any given time on any given night? One way is a planisphere. This is a handheld, adjustable sky chart that needs to be set to your approximate latitude. You rotate its two parts relative to each other depending on date and time.

Another way is using apps. Computer or phone software will show you the night sky for a given date and time, as long as it has your location. See the Resources section for more information.

CONNECTING WITH OTHERS

You can learn about astronomy and observe the night sky all by yourself, but it can be more fun to participate with others. A great way to see things through impressive telescopes is to attend a public star party. These are usually held by local amateur astronomy clubs, which you can also join. Some schools have their own astronomy clubs.

Star party preparing for the night

You can also join a national or international group of space enthusiasts. The largest example is the Planetary Society. And it has an amazing chief scientist. (It's me!) See the Resources section for more information on how to pursue these options.

TYPES OF OBJECTS IN THE NIGHT SKY

In the night sky, you can see stars and identify star patterns with just your eyes. These patterns are called asterisms or constellations. Often, you can see planets. They typically look like bright stars. You can sometimes see Earth satellites crossing the sky, including the International Space Station. The ISS is brighter than the brightest star when it's visible from your location. To find out when you're able to view it in the sky, go to the Resources section. There are also various types of so-called deep sky objects, most of which require binoculars or a telescope to see. These include nebulae, galaxies, and star clusters.

STARS, PLANETS, AND CONSTELLATIONS

An asterism is any group of stars that makes a pattern. A constellation is an official pattern that is internationally agreed upon. There are eighty-eight modern constellations. Constellations also define boundaries in areas of the sky, kind of like the borders of countries on Earth.

Probably the most recognizable asterism in the Northern Hemisphere is the Big Dipper. This collection of seven relatively bright stars is thought to resemble a "dipper," like a soup ladle. It is part of the constellation Ursa Major, also known as the Great Bear. It is always roughly in the north. From most of the Northern Hemisphere, it is visible year-round.

Drawing a line from the two stars at the dipper's end is how you find Polaris, the North Star.

Polaris is the tip of the handle in another asterism, the Little Dipper. It looks like the Big Dipper but is smaller and the stars are dimmer. It is part of the constellation Ursa Minor, also known as Lesser Bear.

Diagram of Cassiopeia constellation

Caph>

Cassiopeia is an easy-to-find constellation. It looks like a *W* or an *M* depending on the season and the time of night. To find it, use the same line from the Big Dipper and continue it past the North Star. You will reach one end of Cassiopeia, a star named Caph.

Venus, Jupiter, Mars, Saturn, and Mercury are bright and easy to see, but you have to know where to look because they move around compared to the stars. To know where to find the planets, see the Resources section of this book.

DEEP SKY OBJECTS

Three types of deep sky objects are nebulae, star clusters, and galaxies. They usually require binoculars or a telescope, but some are visible with just your eyes.

A nebula is a huge cloud of dust and gas in space. One can be spotted in the constellation Orion. This is one of the easiest constellations to identify in the winter evening sky in the northern hemisphere. Particularly identifiable is Orion's Belt, three similarly bright stars that are evenly spaced in a line. Below that are three dimmer stars, forming Orion's Sword. The middle of those three stars is actually the Orion Nebula.

Hubble Space Telescope image of Orion Nebula

A star cluster is a group of stars that are near each other in three-dimensional space. The Pleiades, a group of relatively young stars that formed in the same region of

Pleiades, a star cluster

space, is the easiest star cluster to identify in the sky with just your eyes. It can be found by drawing a line through Orion's Belt and following it to a clump of medium-brightness stars that are near each other.

A galaxy is a collection of hundreds of thousands to trillions of stars held together by their mutual gravity. We live in the Milky Way galaxy. The Andromeda galaxy is the closest galaxy of similar size to the Milky Way. Even though it is 2.5 million light-years away, you can see it with just your eyes. It is visible as a fuzzy patch in the constellation Andromeda. That fuzzy patch looks brighter and bigger in binoculars or a telescope.

MESSIER OBJECTS

Many of the night-sky objects have a name and a number. For example, the Andromeda galaxy is M31.

In the 1700s, a French astronomer named Charles Messier cataloged and numbered the fuzzy-looking objects he could see in the sky with or without his telescope. He ended up with 110 numbered objects. Although he didn't fully realize it, these objects are a combination of galaxies, nebulae, and star clusters. The numbers are now called Messier numbers. Amateur astronomers will sometimes keep track of how many Messier objects they have seen, and sometimes there are observing marathons to try to see as many as possible in one night.

Andromeda galaxy, taken with an amateur telescope

Messier objects include the Orion Nebula (M42) and the Pleiades (M45) as well as the Whirlpool galaxy (M51), which is near the tip of the handle of the Big Dipper and is best seen with a telescope.

EARTH-ORBITING SATELLITES

About 5,000 active satellites orbit the Earth. Most of the satellites are in what is called low Earth orbit, which is about 110 miles (180 kilometers) altitude to 1,250 miles (2,000 kilometers) altitude. There is also

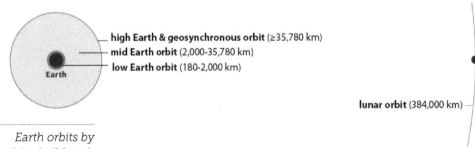

high **Earth & geosynchronous orbit** (≥35,780 km)
mid **Earth orbit** (2,000-35,780 km)
low **Earth orbit** (180-2,000 km)

Earth

lunar orbit (384,000 km)

Earth orbits by altitude (Moon's orbit for scale)

the geostationary orbit, which is over the equator at about 22,500 miles (36,000 kilometers) altitude. There, a satellite's orbital period is the same as the Earth's rotation—roughly one day. A spacecraft in that orbit stays over the same place on Earth all the time. Everything between low Earth orbit and geostationary orbit is referred to as medium Earth orbit or mid Earth orbit.

The number of active satellites is increasing faster than ever before. Companies are launching thousands over a few years as "Internet providers." Astronomers are concerned that these "megaconstellations" of satellites in low Earth orbit will interfere with scientific observations.

BEYOND THE BACKYARD: OBSERVATORIES

Observatories are places with permanent telescope facilities. Professional telescopes are usually placed on top of mountains to get above as much of the atmosphere as possible for better observations. Structures, often

The SOAR Telescope dome in Chile

dome-shaped, house the telescope to protect it from bad weather and keep the temperature stable.

Planetariums are educational facilities tied to space and science. They often have observatories with large telescopes that are available for public viewings.

More and more, observations are taken remotely as astronomers operate the telescope through the Internet. As a member of the public, you can subscribe to services that allow you to remotely operate their telescopes at various places around the world.

BECOME AN EXPLORER

There is so much wild and wonderful stuff to learn about our solar system. And there's so much more that humanity will learn in the future. We live in an incredibly exciting time for space exploration and astronomy. The future will see new generations of the world's largest telescopes, including space telescopes. New robotic space missions are being launched to the incredible worlds of our solar system. Humans are preparing to voyage into farther regions of space. New amazing discoveries, surprises, and knowledge are always just around the corner. Get excited, get exploring, and enjoy space!

GLOSSARY

asteroid: small rocky or metallic object in space

astronomical unit (AU): average distance between the Earth and the Sun, about 93 million miles (150 million kilometers)

astronomy: the study of anything in space, typically using telescopes

atmosphere: gases held by gravity to a planet, moon, or other body

axis: imaginary line around which a body rotates

comet: object in space made of ice and dirt that gives off dust and gas to form tails when it comes near the Sun

convection: process in which heat is transferred by the movement of fluid

core: innermost portion of the Sun, the Moon, or a planet

dwarf planet: round object that goes around the Sun but does not orbit another object; unlike a planet, it has objects close to the same size near its orbit

dwarf star: star of relatively small size and low luminosity

electromagnetic spectrum: range of wavelengths over which electromagnetic radiation, or light, extends

ellipse: mathematical shape similar to a squished circle or oval

equatorial plane: imaginary flat surface running through the equator of a planetary body

exosphere: outermost layer of a planetary body's atmosphere

gas: state of matter that has no fixed shape and no fixed volume

giant planets: Jupiter, Saturn, Uranus, and Neptune in our solar system

gravity: force acting between objects that gets stronger with greater mass

lander: spacecraft designed to land on the surface of a planet, moon, or other planetary body

light-year: the distance light travels in space in one year, about 5.9 trillion miles or 9.5 trillion kilometers

magnetosphere: volume of space where a planetary body's magnetic field is dominant

microbial life: microscopic organisms, such as bacteria

moon: object that orbits a planetary body; a natural satellite

natural satellite: another term for a moon

nuclear fusion: when two nuclei get squished together to form a heavier nucleus, releasing a huge amount of energy

orbit: path a planet or other object follows as it goes around another object; also, to go around another object

phenomena: interesting things that can be observed and studied

photon: particle of light

planet: big ball-shaped object that goes around the Sun but does not orbit another object; a planet does not have anything close to its same size near its orbit

plasma: state of matter similar to an electrically charged filled gas

plate tectonics: theory that Earth's outer layer is divided into large plates that slide over Earth's mantle

red giant: end phase of a star's life in which the star expands and its surface cools, causing the red color

ring system: disc or ring of material that orbits a planet

rocky planets: another term for terrestrial planets; Mercury, Venus, Earth, and Mars in our solar system

sidereal day: one rotation of a planetary body relative to the distant stars

solar day: one rotation of a planetary body relative to the Sun; what we normally call a day

solar flare: intense, temporary brightening of a specific area on the Sun

solar wind: outflow of charged particles from the Sun

spectroscopy: using the detailed colors of light to learn what things are made of

sunspots: dark, temporary areas on the Sun that are cooler than their surroundings

terrestrial planets: another term for rocky planets; Mercury, Venus, Earth, and Mars in our solar system

trans-Neptunian objects: objects that spend most of their orbits beyond the orbit of Neptune

universe: all of space and everything in it

vacuum: area that does not have any matter

white dwarf: what is left at the end of the lives of most stars; they are much smaller than stars but have similar mass

RESOURCES

GENERAL SPACE EXPLORATION

NASA
NASA.gov
NASA has extensive resources, including dates you can observe upcoming eclipses, information on space-related careers, and Spot the Station, which lets you enter your location to find when the International Space Station (ISS) will be visible flying overhead. Search "NASA/JPL Night Sky Network" to discover astronomy clubs in your area.

The Planetary Society
Planetary.org
The world's largest space interest group that you have the option to join. You can find information and updates on all things space as well as a guide to future total solar eclipses.

Random Space Facts

RandomSpaceFact.com

Author Bruce Betts's website offers information and links to his other astronomy-related content, including videos, podcasts, books, classes, and social media.

WHERE AND WHEN TO LOOK FOR PLANETS

Astronomy

Astronomy.com

Check out "The Sky This Week," a daily digest of celestial events occurring in the weeks to come.

Sky and Telescope

SkyandTelescope.org

Check out "This Week's Sky at a Glance" for info on what you can observe in the sky over the course of the week. You can also find local astronomy clubs here.

Stellarium

Stellarium.org

Stellarium is free night sky software for PC, Mac, or Linux. Make sure to set your city as the default location when you use it. Many paid software programs also exist.

OTHER

American Meteor Society

AMSMeteors.org

This nonprofit scientific organization was established in 1911 to support and encourage both professional and amateur astronomers. Check out its Meteor

Shower Calendar to discover where and when you can spot the most active and easiest to observe meteor showers.

The Astronomical League

Astroleague.org/astronomy-clubs-usa-state
Find information about local astronomy clubs across the United States.

Bureau of Labor Statistics

BLS.gov
Search for "Career Exploration," and you'll find a page of student resources. Under "science," you can learn about how to become an astronomer, median wages, and similar jobs and find resources by state.

Heavens Above

Heavens-Above.com
The site has predictions for when you can spot satellites. Make sure to enter your city to get the most accurate information. You'll also find sky charts and much more.

INDEX

ACKNOWLEDGMENTS

Thanks to Jennifer Vaughn for her guidance, love, and support and to my sons, Daniel and Kevin Betts, for bringing happiness and fulfillment to my life. Thanks to my parents, Bert A. and Barbara Lang Betts, Kathleen Reagan Betts, and Kyrsten Proctor for all their support. Thanks to Bill Nye and the staff of the Planetary Society for their support of my broader education efforts. Thanks to my editor, Julie Haverkate, and to the rest of the Callisto Media team for making this book become a book.

ABOUT THE AUTHOR

 **Dr. Bruce Betts** is a planetary scientist and children's book author who loves teaching people about planets, space, and the night sky in fun and entertaining ways. He is the author of *Astronomy for Kids*, *Super Cool Space Facts*, *My First Book of Planets*, *Space Exploration for Kids*, and *V.R. Space Explorers: Titan's Black Cat*.

Dr. Betts has lots of college degrees, lots of big dogs, and two sons. He is the chief scientist and LightSail program manager for the world's largest space interest group, the Planetary Society. He has a BS and an MS from Stanford and a planetary science PhD from Caltech. His research there and at the Planetary Science Institute focused on infrared studies of planetary surfaces. He managed planetary instrument development programs at NASA Headquarters. Follow him on Twitter @RandomSpaceFact and Facebook.com/DrBruceBetts or check out his website: randomspacefact.com.